THE KINSALE

COOKBOOK

Recipes from Renowned Chefs and Residents of Kinsale, Ireland

Dearest Bridey,
Happy Baking

love

Kathryn

xxx

KINSALE
COOKBOOK

Illustrations
Deirdre Mullins

Printer
Rogers Printing, Inc.
2001

With sincere thanks
to all who so graciously
responded to the call.

Jane Bergin

A SHORT HISTORY

Kinsale, because of its land-locked harbour and its location on the Southern Irish coast, has been a well-known port for over a thousand years. In 1965, it became the first town in Ireland to be awarded the Flag of the Council of Europe in recognition of its Europeans over the centuries. It might equally have been identified in a world-wide contest in both the old and the new worlds.

Of course it attracted invaders and so the harbour was fortified over a long period. In Irish history it is best known for three events. First the Spanish landing of 1601, followed by the hundred days siege and the battle of 1602. Then there was the landing of King James II in 1689, and finally Marlbough's siege of 1690.

During the 19th century fishing was a major industry. Spring mackerel fishing brought boats from the Isle of Man, England, Scotland and France as well as many parts of Ireland amounting in all to some eight hundred boats. The autumn mackerel fishing specialized in sending barreled salt mackerel to America.

Quite another aspect of life in the town was the making of the famous Kinsale lace which centered on the Convent of Mercy. The first superior, Mother M. Francis Bridgeman, is also remembered through having led a group of nursing nuns to war-torn Crimea in 1854.

Shipbuilding and its associated crafts loom large in the history of Kinsale also. One of the more famous ships built at Kinsale was that of the HMS Kinsale in 1700 which mounted 32 guns. An earlier ship was the prefabulated vessel which "sailed over the mountains" and captured Ross Castle, Killarney in 1652. Thomas Chudleigh the elder, is buried in St. Multose Church where his wooden monument is made from planks of the famous vessel.

Not far away in the churchyard, were buried some of the victims from the Cunard luxury liner Lusitania, torpedoed off the Old Head of Kinsale, her first and last landfall, on 7 May, 1915.

Today, many tourists bend their steps towards Kinsale, not only for its history and charm but also for its reputation as being the gourmet capital of Ireland.

Michael Mulcahy

TABLE OF CONTENTS

Hor d'ouvres & Drinks

Wine Museum

PARMA HAM
with ARTICHOKE HEARTS

1 small tin artichoke hearts
24 slices parma ham
1 oz (25ml) sherry vinegar
2 oz (50ml) olive oil
¼ red bell pepper, finely diced
salt and pepper
chives

Drain and quarter the artichokes. In a round bowl, whisk the sherry vinegar and seasoning until well combined. Then slowly whisk in the olive oil. Toss the artichokes in sherry vinaigrette and arrange in the centre of a plate. Fold the parma ham slices to make cones and arrange around the artichokes. Garnish with diced pepper and chives.

Urban & Jackie Mutter
Old Head Golf Link Restaurant

GOLDEN FRIED PARCELS
of CASHEL BLUE CHEESE

2 wedges Cashel blue cheese, stilton or Danish blue
filo pastry sheets
green tomato relish
   (White House or other good quality farmhouse relish)

Wrap 2-3oz (50-100g) portions individually in a sheet of filo pastry. Seal the filo with either egg yolk or water. Deep fry at 190C/375F until golden. Meanwhile, gently heat the relish. To serve, place the hot cheese parcel on warmed relish. Garnish with lemon slices.

Note: *I find the citron taste goes well with the blue cheese and the sweet relish.*

Mark Russell
The White House

3

BACON-WRAPPED PRUNES

¼ cup (55g) raisins, soaked overnight in
1 teas dark rum and water just to cover
¼ cup (55g) cream cheese
16 large prunes
1 cup (250ml) dry red wine
8 bacon slices

Preheat oven 190C/375F. Drain raisins and discard rum and water. Purée raisins and cream cheese in a small blender or mix with a fork, mashing the raisins. Simmer the prunes in wine about 10 minutes. Cool. Fill the prunes with the raisin and cream cheese mixture. Don't overstuff, as cream cheese mixture will run out the sides. Wrap half a slice of bacon around each stuffed prune and secure with a toothpick. Bake on a cookie sheet until the bacon is brown and crisp, about 12 minutes turning once. Drain on paper towels. Serve warm. **Yield: 16 nibbles.**

Anonymous

ORANGE & YELLOW PEPPERS
with a BRIOCHE FILLING

2 each, orange and yellow peppers
3 oz (85g) brioche crumbs (3-4 thick slices)
1 oz (25g) pine nuts, toasted & roughly chopped
handful each, flat leaf parsley and mint
9 oz (250g) haloumi cheese
zest of 1 lemon
handful black olives, optional
2 Tbsp (30ml) extra virgin olive oil
sea salt and ground black pepper

Preheat oven to 190C/375F. Put the whole orange and yellow peppers in a roasting tin and bake for 45 minutes until soft. Put the brioche crumbs on to a baking sheet and toast them in the oven turning now and then, for 5 minutes or until golden and crisp.
Put the toasted crumbs in a bowl. Add the pine nuts, herbs, cheese, lemon zest, olives and half of the olive oil. Mix together and season to taste. Remove the stalks from the peppers and scoop out the seeds. Fill the peppers with crumb mixture and drizzle over the remaining olive oil. Bake for 15 minutes or until warmed through. **Yield: 4 servings.**

Suggestion: *Change to green peppers for St. Patrick's Day*

Ann Fitzsimons

PATÉ

8 oz (225g) chicken livers, finely chopped
2 pieces streaky bacon, chopped
1 small onion, finely chopped
1 clove garlic, minced
3 oz (85g) butter
½ teas savory
1 Tbls parsley
2 Tbls brandy

Melt the butter in a sauté pan over medium heat.
Add the onion plus the garlic and sauté gently for a few minutes. Then add all the remaining ingredients except for the brandy and cook between 7-7 minutes. Remove from the stove and cool. When cool, incorporate the brandy and then put the entire mixture through a kitchen mincer. Store the paté in a container and seal with melted butter. Refrigerate until serving.

Nuala Casey

ITALIAN STUFFED MUSHROOMS

12 large, fresh mushrooms
2 Tbsp butter
1 sweet Italian sausage, minced (about 2½ oz or 70g)
1 small clove garlic, minced
¼ teas salt
8 oz (225g) dry bread crumbs
1 Tbsp (15ml) Marsala or sweet sherry
2 Tbsp (30ml) water
olive oil
1 oz (25g) freshly grated Parmesan cheese

Stem the mushrooms and wipe caps with a damp cloth. Melt butter in a skillet; add sausage and garlic. Cook over medium heat for about 10 minutes, breaking up the sausage and stirring often. Remove from heat. Stir in the remaining ingredients except cheese. Blend well. Brush the mushroom caps with olive oil and place cap side down on a cookie sheet. Stuff the caps with the sausage mixture, sprinkle with cheese, and grill about 5 inches from the heat for 10 minutes, or until sizzling hot.

Jacqueline Dubois

GARLIC MUSHROOMS

1 ¼ lb (550g) large, even-sized mushrooms
8 oz (225g) butter or margarine
2 cloves garlic, peeled, and chopped
1 Tbsp (15ml) lemon juice
2 Tbsp chopped parsley
Salt
Black pepper, freshly ground
1 3oz (85g) white breadcrumbs for topping

Preheat oven to 180C/350F. Wipe the mushrooms with kitchen paper and remove the stalks to keep for soups or sauces. To make the filling, cream the butter, garlic and lemon juice together. Stir in the chopped parsley and add seasoning to taste. Spread the filling generously into each mushroom cap. Place the mushrooms skin side down in a large gratin dish. Sprinkle the breadcrumbs evenly over the top. Cook 15-20 minutes until sizzling and the crumbs are golden and crisp. Sprinkle with chopped parsley before serving.

Tony Santry

MULLED WINE

2 bottles dry red wine
4 oz (115g) brown sugar
12 whole cloves
4 cinnamon sticks
Peel of 1 large orange, cut into long strips
Peel of 1 large lemon, cut into long strips
2 cups (500ml) port
2 cups (500ml) brandy

Combine all ingredients except port and brandy in a large pot (not aluminum). Simmer for 10 minutes, stirring occasionally. Add brandy and port and heat until steaming – not boiling as you will boil off the alcohol!

MULLED WINE II

1 bottle red wine
6 cloves
3 cinnamon sticks
Orange, lemon and apple slices
Brown sugar to taste
½ pint (300ml) orange juice
½ pint (300ml) lemonade
¼ pint (150ml) brandy

Combine all ingredients except brandy. Simmer 10-15 minutes. Add brandy

Note: Taste as you go along and the final outcome no longer matters!

Mary Lawrence

SOUPS & CHOWDER

Scilly

FRENCH ONION SOUP

4 ox (115g) butter
6 onions (about 3 lbs (1.3kg) sliced
6 cloves garlic, sliced
½ cup (125ml) dry white wine
3 cups (750ml) chicken broth
3 cups (750ml) beef broth
1 teas Dijon mustard

4 French bread slices, toasted
1 cup grated Swiss cheese
4½ oz (125g) Parmesan cheese

Melt butter in a large, heavy saucepan over medium heat. Add onions and garlic and sauté until very tender and brown, about 45 minutes. Add wine and simmer until reduced to glaze, about 45 minutes. Stir in chicken broth, beef broth and mustard. Simmer 20 minutes. Season to taste with salt and pepper. Preheat grill. Ladle soup into ovenproof bowls. Top each with a slice of toast and grated cheeses. Grill until cheeses melt and bubble.

Note: Can be prepared 1 day ahead. Refrigerate. Return soup to simmer before continuing.

Jacqueline Dubois

MUSHROOM SOUP

½ lb (225g) mushrooms
1 onion
2 oz (50g) butter
1 oz (25g) flour
8 oz (225ml) white stock
1 potato
1 teas (5ml) Soya Sauce
salt and black pepper
¼ cup (60ml) milk

Melt 1oz (25g) butter in a saucepan. Gently simmer chopped onion and potato. Add chopped mushrooms and stock. Cook for 15 minutes. Meanwhile make a roux. Melt the remaining butter. Add the flour and cook for 2 minutes. Add the roux, Soya Sauce, milk and the soup together in a blender and purée. Season to taste with salt and pepper.

Sheila Ryan

TOMATO & CHEESE SOUP

1 oz (25g) butter
2 large onions
plain flour
2 lbs (900g) tomatoes, skinned, seeded and chopped
1 clove garlic, crushed
1 sprig fresh rosemary
1 sprig thyme
1 pint (600ml) chicken stock (may use a cube)
salt and pepper
8 oz (225ml) cream
1 egg yolk
4 oz (115g) grated Gruyère cheese

Melt the butter in a saucepan. Add the onion and cook without browning for 10 minutes. Stir in the flour and simmer for another few minutes. Stir in the tomatoes, garlic, herbs, stock and salt and pepper to taste. Bring to a boil, cover and simmer for 30 minutes or until the tomatoes are very tender. Cool slightly and liquidize until smooth. Return to pan. Blend the cream and egg yolk together; stir into pan. Heat through gently. Do not boil or the soup will curdle. Stir in the cheese and serve immediately.

Ann Marie Searls

MEDITERRANEAN VEGETABLE SOUP

1 cup (222g) white beans
3-4 pieces bacon, chopped
½ cup (125ml) olive oil
1-2 medium onions, chopped
1 cup (225g) diced carrots
1 cup (225g) green beans, uncooked, cut up
2 stalks celery, chopped
2 cans chopped tomatoes or 2 cups fresh
3 cups (675g) shredded green cabbage
1 clove garlic
1 Tbsp parsley
1 teas dried rosemary
Bay leaf
9 oz (250g) elbow macaroni
Parmesan cheese

Soak beans overnight and boil the next day until the skins pop, about 30 minutes. Drain beans in a colander. In a sauté pan, cook the bacon, drain the fat. Add olive oil, then the onions and cook, stirring often, until clear. Add the carrots, celery and the green beans. Sauté for 3-5 minutes. Transfer to soup pan. Add tomatoes, cabbage and herbs. Cover with water. Bring to boil, then simmer a minimum of 1½ hours. Add cooked macaroni at the last moment. Serve with Parmesan cheese.

Louise Hayes

SMOKED CHOWDER

½ lb (225g) cod fillet, bones removed and cut into 1" cubes
½ lb (225g) smoked cod, bones removed & cut in 1" cubes
4 streaky rashers, cut into strips
1 large onion, diced
2 cloves garlic, finely chopped
1 yellow pepper, finely diced
1 red chili pepper, de-seeded & finely chopped
3 large potatoes, diced
4½ cups (1 litre) fish stock
9 oz (250ml) milk
9 oz (250ml) cream
4 oz (115g) plain flour
Ground black pepper & salt to season
Tabasco
Spring onion to garnish

In a large stockpot, melt the butter over a medium heat. Add the onions, peppers, garlic and celery. Sauté until onions are transparent. Add flour and cook gently, stirring constantly. Add the fish stock and potatoes and simmer for 15 minutes. Gradually add in the milk and cream concurrently, then remove from heat. Season to taste. In a separate pan, sauté the strips of bacon, and put to one side. Serve in a large bowl, topped with bacon strips and spring onions. Splash with tabasco for a bit of spice!!!

Michelle Donohoe
Janey Mac's

CUCUMBER SOUP

1 large cucumber, peeled and chopped
2 oz (50g) chopped onion
1 oz (25g) margarine
1 oz (25g) flour
½ pint (300ml) milk
1 pint (600ml) stock

Simmer vegetables in stock for 30 minutes. Make a roux with margarine and flour. Leave to cool. Add to soup. Liquidise. Add milk. Bring to the boil and cook for 5 minutes, stirring all the time.

CHILLED CUCUMBER SOUP

1 large cucumber
½ green pepper, seeded and chopped
1 pint (600ml) chicken stock
¾ cup (170ml) commercial sour cream
1 Tbsp (15ml) lemon juice
few drops tabasco sauce
1 Tbsp fresh chopped dill or 2 teas dried
salt

Peel the cucumber. Split lengthwise and scoop out the seeds with a spoon. Chop cucumber flesh into chunks and place in a liquidiser or food processor together with the other ingredients. Process until well pureed. Taste and add salt if needed. Chill.

Michael Reese
Old Bank House

BREADS & PASTA

the Courthouse

DARK BROWN BREAD

1 ½ lb (675g) wholemeal flour
½ lb (225g) white flour
2 oz (55g) oat flakes
3 oz (85g) sesame seeds
3 oz (85g) sunflower seeds
3 oz (85g) pin head oatmeal
8 oz (225ml) black treacle molasses
3 eggs
2 Tbls butter
2 teas salt
2 teas bread soda
4½ cups (1 litre) buttermilk

Preheat oven to 200C/400F. Put flours, oat flakes, sesame seeds, sunflower seeds, bread soda, and salt into a large mixing bowl. Whip the eggs, and together with the buttermilk, stir into the dry ingredients. Then add the treacle and the butter, which has been melted, then cooled. Stir all together. Pour into 4 2lb tins and place in oven. After 15-20 minutes, turn the oven down to 180C/350F and bake approximately 35 minutes.

Michael Reese
Old Bank House

CRACKPOTS
BROWN BREAD

1½ lbs (675g) brown flour
8 oz (225g) white flour
1 teas bread soda
½ teas salt
2 Tbls pinhead oatmeal
1 teas sesame seeds
1 Tbls caraway seeds
1 egg
¾ cup (175ml) oil
16 oz (450ml) buttermilk
2 Tbls (30ml) treacle

Preheat oven to 200F/100C.

Mix the dry ingredients, add the wet ones, mix well. Bake for 45 minutes. Can be varied with different seeds or nuts.

Vickie McGlennon
Crackpots Ceramic Restaurant

PHIL PRICE'S BROWN BREAD

2 lb (900g) wheatmeal flour
4 oz (115g) bran
2 oz (55g) wheat germ
4 oz (115g) muesli
2 teas bread soda
1 egg
2 teas (30ml) treacle or more
1 pint (600ml) buttermilk

Preheat oven to 200C/400F.

Mix all the ingredients so that they are moist and sticking together. Grease and flour 3 1-lb bread pans. Place in oven for 30 minutes, then reduce the temperature to 150C/350F for another 15 minutes. Once out of the oven, wrap in a tea towel to cool and enjoy.

Phil Price
Danabel Bed & Breakfast

TREACLE & WALNUT SODA BREAD

12 oz (350g) wholemeal flour
4 oz (115g) plain flour
1 teas salt
1 teas bread soda
¼ cup (60ml) oil
1 pint (600ml) buttermilk
4 chopped walnuts
2 teas (10ml) black treacle

Preheat oven to 200C/400F.

Mix all the ingredients together. Bake in a greased bread tin for 1 hour. Cool on a wire rack for ½ hour. Serve.

Richard Ennos

The Little Skillet

SODA BREAD or SCONES

1½ lbs (675g) brown wholemeal flour (preferable stone-ground)
1 lb (450g) white flour
1 oz (25g) fine oatmeal
1 egg (optional)
2 teas bread soda
1½ pints (850ml) buttermilk, approximately
3 oz (85g) butter

Preheat oven to 230C/450F. Mix dry ingredients well together. Rub in butter. Make a well in the centre and add the beaten egg, then immediately add most of the buttermilk. Working from the centre, mix with your hands, adding more milk as necessary. The dough should be soft but not sticky. Turn out on a floured board and knead lightly, just enough to shape into a round. Flatten slightly to about 2 inches. Put on a baking sheet and with a knife mark with a deep cross. Bake for 15-20 minutes, then reduce heat to 200C/400F and bake another 20-25 minutes or until it sounds hollow when tapped.

Peggy Arundel

BOXTY BREAD

1 lb (450g) raw potatoes
1 lb (450g) flour (4 cups)
1 lb (450g) mashed potatoes (2 cups)
4 oz (115ml) melted butter or bacon fat

Preheat oven to 150C/300F. Peel the raw potatoes and grate on to a clean cloth. Wring them tightly over a basin, catching the liquid. Put the grated potatoes into another basin and spread with the cooked mashed potatoes. When the starch has sunk to the bottom of the raw potato liquid, pour off the water and scrape the starch on to the potatoes. Mix well. Sift the flour, salt and pepper over it. Finally add the melted butter or fat. Knead. Roll out on a floured board and shape into 4 round cakes. Make a cross over the top of each. Cook on a greased baking sheet for about 40 minutes. Serve hot, split in 2 with butter.

Mary Austin

SPECIALTY of the HOUSE
BUTTERMILK PANCAKES

3 eggs, separated
2 cups (500ml) buttermilk
2 cups (450g) flour
1 teas bread soda
1 Tbsp sugar
¼ cup (50ml) unsalted butter, melted
oil or butter

Beat the egg yolks in a large bowl until light and lemon coloured. Slowly stir in the buttermilk. With a wooden spoon, stir in the flour, soda and sugar being careful not to overwork. Small lumps will disappear during the cooking. Stir in the melted butter. Beat the egg whites until stiff but not dry. Fold into the pancake mixture. Heat griddle or cast-iron skillet over medium heat until hot. Grease lightly with oil or butter. Pour about 1/3 cup (75ml) batter for each pancake onto the griddle. Cook until bubbles form on top and undersides are nicely browned, about 1 minute. Turn pancake over and brown the other side. Either serve at once or keep warm in a 100C/200F oven, un-stacked, until the remaining cakes are cooked. **Yields about 12 4" pancakes.**

Nell Schick

COFFEE CAKE

6 oz (175g) butter or margarine at room temperature
6 oz (175g) castor (superfine) sugar
3 large eggs
6 oz (175 g) self-raising flour, sieved
1 Tbsp (15ml) coffee essence

Preheat oven to 180C/350F.

Grease two 6½ or 7½" sandwich tins (16 or 19 cm). Place all the ingredients in a mixing bowl and beat with a wooden spoon until well mixed (2 to 3 minutes). Divide the mixture into the 2 tins and bake for 25-35 minutes. Turn out and cool on a wire rack.

Coffee Icing
3 oz (85g) butter or margarine
8 oz (225 g) icing (powdered) sugar, sieved
1 Tbsp (15ml) coffee essence
1 Tbsp (15ml) milk

Place all the ingredients together in a mixing bowl and beat with a wooden spoon until smooth. To finish the cake, sandwich the two cakes with a little of the icing. Pipe the remaining icing on top. Serve.

Elma O'Donoghue

MEDITERRANEAN PIZZA

Pizza Base
½ oz (15g) compressed yeast
½ teas sugar
½ cup (125ml) lukewarm water
1½ cups (350ml) flour
pinch of salt
2 Tbsp (30ml) oil

Filling
2 teas (10ml) oil
1 onion
1 clove garlic
14 oz (400g) can whole tomatoes
1 Tbls tomato paste
½ teas oregano
½ teas basil
1 teas sugar
salt and pepper

Topping
4 oz (115g) feta cheese
2 oz (55g) mozzarella cheese, grated
2 oz (55g) black olives
1 large tomato, sliced
6 oz (175g) spinach, chopped
a little garlic

Pizza Base

Stir yeast with sugar, add lukewarm water and let stand for 10 minutes or so. Sift flour and salt into a bowl. Make a well in the centre. Add oil and yeast mixture. Mix to a firm dough. Turn dough onto a floured surface, knead for 10 minutes or until dough is smooth and elastic. Place in a lightly oiled bowl, cover, and stand in a warm place for 30 minutes, or until the dough has doubled in bulk. Knock the dough down, knead into a smooth ball. Flatten into a circle about 1 inch (2.5cm) thick. Roll out from centre to edge to fit a 10inch (25cm) pizza pan.

Filling

Heat oil in a pan, add peeled and finely chopped onion. Cook until onion is transparent. Add crushed garlic, undrained mashed tomatoes and the remaining ingredients. Bring sauce to boil, reduce heat and simmer uncovered, stirring occasionally for 10-15 minutes or until sauce is thick and smooth. Cool. Spread cooked filling over the pizza base. Combine grated feta and mozzarella and sprinkle half over the pizza. Top with approximately 6 slices of tomato, spinach, olives and garlic. Sprinkle remaining cheese over the top. Bake in hot oven 15 minutes or until the crust is golden brown. **Serves 2-3.**

Brett & Avril Malone

Café Palermo

CABBAGE & PASTA SNAILS

2¼ lb (1kg) cabbage
7 oz (200g) onions
1 clove garlic
sugar
white wine vinegar
salt and pepper
a few caraway seeds
5 oz (150g) peeled potatoes
3½ fl oz (100ml) white wine
1-2 Tbls (15-30g) flour
3 oz (70g) butter
7 oz (200g) crème fraîche
4 oz (100g) Milleens cheese

Pasta
10 oz (300g) plain white flour
2 eggs
3 egg yolks
1 Tbsp (15ml) olive oil
pinch salt

Place the flour in a food processor and switch the machine on. Add the eggs and the egg yolks. When all the egg has been amalgamated, add the olive oil and salt and mix briefly. Remove from the machine and knead for a few minutes on a lightly floured surface. Cover with cling film and allow it to rest.

Quarter the cabbage lengthwise, remove the stalk and cut into fine julienne. Finely chop the onions and garlic. Dissolve sugar in water, add white wine vinegar and the cabbage. Season with salt, pepper and caraway. Cook gently at low heat for 10 minutes. Add potatoes and white wine and cook for another 15 minutes. In the meantime, roll out the pasta dough with the help of a pasta machine, until Mark 5 on the machine (15 X 28 cm). Preheat the oven to 180C/350F and butter a large gratin dish. Spread the cabbage mixture on to the pasta. Roll and cut into 1½ inch (4cm) thick pieces. Put the rolls next to each other standing into the gratin dish and cover with the crème fraîche and the grated cheese. Bake for 45 minutes.

Michael Relja
Casino House

BOLOGNESE MEAT SAUCE

4 Tbls unsalted butter
4 Tbls (60ml) olive oil
1 medium onion, chopped
2 celery stalks, chopped
1 small carrot, scraped and chopped
1 lb (450g) minced beef
½ teas salt
1 cup (225ml) white wine
½ cup (125ml) milk
Generous pinch of freshly grated nutmeg
1½ lbs (700g) ripe tomatoes, peeled and chopped
or 2 cans chopped

Heat the butter and olive oil over medium heat and sauté the onion for several minutes or until soft. Add the celery and carrot and cook very gently for 2-3 minutes. Add the minced meat, breaking it up with a fork, and cook just until all of the redness is gone. Stir in salt and wine. Raise heat to moderately high and cook until the wine has completely evaporated, stirring frequently. Reduce heat to medium, add the milk and the nutmeg and cook until the milk has evaporated.

Now add the tomatoes and stir for several minutes, so ingredients are thoroughly blended. When the sauce starts to bubble, reduce the heat as low as possible, so the sauce barely simmers. Continue cooking, uncovered, for at least 3 hours. It should be watched fairly steadily during this time. Taste and correct seasoning. Serve over spaghetti or other pasta. **Serves 6.**

Anonymous

SPINACH SAUCE
for FRESH PASTA

10 oz (280g) frozen spinach
3 oz (85g) fresh prosciutto or Parma ham, sliced
2 cloves garlic
1 knob butter
half a handful of pine nuts
half a glass of white wine
13 oz (375ml) cream

Soften ham in garlic and butter. Add white wine and reduce. Add spinach and warm through.   Add cream and warm through. Do not reduce for more than 2 minutes. Add pine nuts. Serve over pasta.

Note: Fresh pasta should be firm after it is cooked.   This will require only about 2 minutes of cooking.

Brett & Avril Malone
Café Palermo

TORTELLINI with
MUSHROOM & BRANDY SAUCE

16 oz (450g) fresh or dried cheese tortellini
½ cup (125ml) freshly grated Parmesan cheese

Sauce
2 Tbsp butter
2 cloves garlic, finely chopped
1 small onion, finely chopped
8 oz (225g) fresh mushrooms, thinly sliced
½ cup (125ml) brandy
4 cups (1 litre) heavy cream
½ teas freshly grated nutmeg
½ teas pepper

Heat butter in a 10" skillet over medium-high heat. Sauté garlic and onion in butter. Stir in mushrooms. Sauté 5 minutes. Stir in brandy. Heat to boiling. Carefully ignite. Stir in whipping cream, nutmeg and pepper when flame dies out. Heat to boiling; reduce heat. Simmer, uncovered 20 minutes, stirring frequently, until thickened. Keep warm while preparing pasta. Cook the tortellini as directed on package; drain. Mix tortellini and sauce; top with cheese. Serve with freshly ground pepper if desired.

Anonymous

GOATS CHEESE RAVIOLI
with TOMATO SAUCE

10 oz (280g) goats cheese
5 oz (140g) ricotta cheese
1 Tbsp fresh chives
1 Tbsp fresh thyme
2 cups (1 lb) plain flour
3 eggs
2 teas (10ml) olive oil

Tomato Sauce
14 oz (400g) can tomatoes
1 Tbsp (15ml) olive oil
1 Tbsp sugar
1 cup (250ml) tomato puree

Combine cheeses and herbs in a bowl, mixing well. Process the flour, eggs and oil until combined. Turn the dough onto a floured surface, press the mixture together and knead until smooth. Cover dough. Refrigerate for 30 minutes. Divide the dough into 4 equal portions. Roll out 1 portion until ½" thick. Place 2 level teas (7ml) of cheese mixture about 2" (5cm) apart on dough. Roll out another portion paper thin, lightly brush with water, and place over filling. Press firmly between the fillings. Cut into square ravioli shapes. Lightly sprinkle with flour. Repeat with remaining pasta and filling. Add ravioli to a pan of boiling water. Simmer, uncovered about 5 minutes or until tender; drain. Serve with tomato sauce.

For the sauce: Mix undrained chopped tomatoes and remaining ingredients together in a pan and simmer uncovered for 10 minutes or until thick.

Serves 4.

Brett & Avril Malone
Café Palermo

CASSEROLES & CRÊPES

the Old Head of Kinsale

ASPARAGUS MOUSSE
with FOIE GRAS

2 lb (400g) asparagus
juice of ½ lemon
one slice toast (to bind the bitter substance)
pinch of salt
pinch of sugar
6 gelatine leaves
4 Tbls(60ml) champagne vinegar
1 Tbls (15ml) raspberry vinegar
1 pint (600ml) cream

Bring 12 cups (1 litre) of water with the salt, sugar and slice of toast to the boil. Add the asparagus and cook until tender. Drain and squeeze through a sieve. Soak the gelatine in cold water for 5 minutes. Squeeze out the water and add to the hot asparagus. Puree. Now stir in the champagne and raspberry vinegar. Add sugar and salt to taste. Leave to cool. Fold in the whipped cream step by step and put into the fridge for at least 3-4 hours.

Next, preheat a frying pan without any oil and pan fry the foie gras. Season with salt, pepper and a little mace. Put aside. Spoon and form some dumplings out of the cold asparagus mousse and put on a plate with the hot foie gras. Spoon over some warm chicken stock. Serve.

Casino House

38

HAM & ASPARAGUS ROLLS

12 slices honey roasted ham
24 tender asparagus tips (tinned work well, too!)
1 pint (600ml) milk
4 oz (115g) Dubliner cheese or your favorite Cheddar
1½ oz (40g) cornflour (cornstarch)
1 tomato, nicely sliced
pinch each of nutmeg, cayenne, salt and pepper
chopped parsley
a little mustard

Preheat oven to 180C/350F. Arrange asparagus between ham and form into rolls. Place in an ovenproof serving dish. To make the sauce, blend the cornflour with a little of the milk until smooth and creamy. Blend in remaining milk and bring to a boil, stirring constantly. Add flavourings and simmer for 1 minute. Stir in ½ of the cheese and pour over the rolls. Top with the remaining cheese and decorate with tomato slices and chopped parsley. Place in oven and cook until golden.

Note: Delicious served with garlic bread and salad.

Rosie Cargin

SESAME TOFU
with SUMMER VEGETABLES

For the Vegetables:
½ Tbsp (7.5ml) olive oil
2 spring onions, chopped
1 clove of garlic, chopped
1 inch ginger, grated
2 Tbsp (30ml) soy sauce
1 Tbsp (15ml) mirin
    (rice wine)
sprinkle of brown sugar
1 teas (5ml) sesame oil
1 Tbsp cashew nuts
1 oz (25g) Chinese
    mushrooms
2 oz (50g) baby carrots
2 oz (50g) mangetout
½ red pepper, sliced
a few broccoli florets
1 leek, sliced
2 oz (50g) bean sprouts

For the Tofu:
1 10oz (280g) block of tofu
Marinade:
2 Tbsp (30ml) soy sauce
½ Tbsp (7.5ml) sesame oil
½ Tbsp (7.5ml) tahini
1 teas (5ml) chili oil
2 spring onions, chopped
ground black pepper

For the Rice:
9 oz (250g) jasmine rice

First, prepare the tofu. Cut the block in three lengthways, then in four widthways, making twelve cubes. Mix together all the marinade ingredients and add to the tofu, turning to coat thoroughly. Allow to marinate for 30 minutes.

Next, rinse the rice in lots of cold water until the cloudy appearance has gone. Put equal measures of rice and water in a pot and jam on the lid using tin foil to prevent any air escaping. Bring to the boil then remove from the heat altogether and let stand for 15 minutes. The rice will the be ready but will keep perfectly for another 30 minutes.

Next, mix together the soy sauce, mirin and sugar and set aside until later. Cover the mushrooms in warm water and after 20 minutes squeeze dry, discard the hard stalks, and chop the caps in two.

Heat a little oil in your wok (or largest frying pan) and quickly fry the cashew nuts. When browned, remove from the pan and drain on kitchen paper. Reserve until later.

Heat remaining oil and add onions, garlic and ginger and stir-fry for about 30 seconds. Add carrots, peppers, leek, and broccoli and fry for 2 minutes, adding some soy sauce or boiling water if required.

At this point, heat a little oil in a small frying pan and add the tofu and fry for 2 or 3 minutes, turning often to ensure each side browns well. At the same time, add the mangetout, mushrooms and soy dressing to the vegetables in the large wok and continue to stir-fry for 2 minutes.

When the tofu is browned, remove to a warm plate and heat the remaining marinade, adding a little water if it seems a bit thick.

To serve, form a bed of rice on one side of the plate, arrange the tofu on top, and pour over a little sauce. On the other side of the plate, arrange the vegetables; scatter with toasted cashew nuts, and finally, sprinkle with some sesame oil. Serve with a good, fruity, Rioja, or, a clean Chablis.

Laura Hayes
Quay Food Company

SAVOURY BAKE

1 medium cauliflower
4 carrots
¼ lb (115g) mushrooms
8 oz (225g) oats
1 package flaked almonds
3 Tbsp (45ml) Soya sauce
2 Tbsp flour
milk
water
oil

Preheat oven to 220C/425F. Chop cauliflower and carrots into medium sized pieces; place in frying pan with a little oil. Fry for a couple of minutes, then add 10oz (300ml) water, and the Soya sauce. Cover and simmer for 10 minutes. Mix together the oats, flaked almonds and enough oil to make the mixture moist in a bowl and leave. Uncover the vegetables, add the mushrooms. Mix the flour with enough milk to make a creamy paste; add Soya sauce to taste. Mix this in with the vegetables. If the mixture is getting too thick, add more milk or water. Empty the vegetable mixture into a deep roasting tin, sprinkle the oat and almond mixture over the top, place in the middle of the oven, and cook for 40 minutes or until browned.

Note: This is nice served with roast potatoes and spinach.

Kate French

AUBERGINE &
GOAT CHEESE BAKE

1 aubergine (eggplant)
3 ripe tomatoes
1 onion, chopped
2 cloves garlic, crushed
1 Tbsp basil leaves, torn
2 teas (10ml) sundried tomato paste
1 teas capers
6 oz (175g) goat cheese, cubed
2 handfuls breadcrumbs
3 Tbsp Parmesan cheese, grated
olive oil
salt and pepper

Tomato Sauce
1 can tomatoes
1 onion, chopped
½ red pepper
2 cloves garlic
basil
vegetable stock

Slice the aubergines lengthways and put on a greased baking tin. Use the bulbous outside for the filling; chip it into small dice. Skin the tomatoes and remove seeds, then dice. Heat some olive oil and fry the onions, diced aubergine, tomatoes and garlic. Add the capers, sundried paste, salt, pepper, and basil. Fry for a few minutes, then leave to cool before adding the cubed goat cheese. When the aubergines are cooked, remove, put a little of the mix into the centre of the sliced aubergines, roll up and place on the baking tray until all gone. Mix the breadcrumbs with the Parmesan and some more basil. Add a bit of olive oil and salt and pepper. Sprinkle breadcrumbs over the aubergines and bake for aapproximately 20 minutes.

For Tomato Sauce: Fry the onion, pepper and garlic in olive oil. Add the tomatoes, basil and vegetable stock. Simmer until the vegetables are soft. Liquidize, adjust seasoning and serve with the bake.

Vickie McGlennon
Crackpots Ceramic Café

SIMPLE VEGETARIAN CURRY

5 medium carrots, chopped
½ medium turnip, chopped
1 medium parsnip, chopped
1 medium lemon, chopped*
1 large apple
1 large onion, diced small
4 cloves garlic, chopped

2 Tbsp (30ml) oil
2 Tbsp (30ml) tomato paste
2 Tbsp (30ml) vinegar
2 Tbsp lentils
2 Tbsp sultanas

1 level teas curry powder
1 level teas coriander
1 level teas cumin
1 level teas garam masala
1 level teas turmeric

1 pint (600ml) water
1 can tomatoes
1 vegetable stock cube
1 teas cardamon seeds (optional)

* The lemon may be chopped whole if organic; otherwise it should be peeled.

Place everything in a large saucepan. Bring to a boil. Cover. Reduce heat to minimum. Simmer about 4 hours or until soft.

Turn off heat. Leave until required. It is particularly good if made first thing in the morning and used for supper.

Reheat gently by placing pan on top of another containing boiling water. Serve with rice.

Attractive extras to accompany this dish are natural yoghurt, pineapple rings, and/or mango chutney.

If a heavy curry is required, at the warm up stage add a package of vegetarian mince such as Quorn or Linda McCartney's, and one can of either chick-peas or haricot beans, drained.

Serves 4.

Croise Brogan

DUBLIN CODDLE

8¼ inch thick ham or bacon slices
4 large onions, sliced
4 Tbsp chopped parsley
2 lbs (1kg) potatoes, peeled and sliced
1 quart (1.2 litres) boiling water
8 port sausages
Salt and pepper

Boil the sausages and bacon or ham (cut into large chunks), in the boiling water for 5 minutes. Drain, but reserve the liquid. Put the meat into a large saucepan (or ovenproof dish) with the thinly sliced onions and potatoes and the chopped parsley. Season to taste and add enough of the stock to barely cover. Lay greaseproof (wax) paper on top and then put on the lid. Simmer gently, or cook in a slow to moderate oven 100C/175F about an hour or until the liquid is reduced by half and all the ingredients are cooked but not mushy. Serve hot with the vegetables on top and fresh soda bread and glasses of Guinness.

Philip McEvoy
The Old Presbytery

COMPANY POTATO
CASSEROLE

6 potatoes
¾ cup butter
1 can cream of chicken (or cream of mushroom) soup
¾ cup sharp Cheddar cheese, shredded
1/3 cup spring onions, chopped
1 carton (250ml) sour cream
½ cup cornflakes, crumbled

Cook the potatoes with skins on. Remove the skins and thin-ly slice the potatoes into a buttered 2½ quart casserole. Mix together ½ cup butter, soup, cheese, green onions and sour cream in a saucepan. Stir over low heat just until heated through and pour over the potatoes. Melt the remaining ¼ cup of butter in a small skillet and add the cornflake crumbs. Mix well. Sprinkle the crumb mixture over the pota-toes. Bake at 180C/350F until bubbly, 35 to 45 minutes. **Serves 10.**

Louise Hayes

LIGHTLY BAKED PANCAKE filled with CHICKEN, MUSHROOMS & BACON

Crêpes (pancake) mix
7 oz (200g) flour
4 eggs
1 pint (600ml) milk
3½ oz (100g) butter, melted
salt
Put all into a bowl and mix until liquified.

Filling
4½ cups (1 litre) chicken stock
½ pint (300ml) cream
7 oz (200g) sliced mushrooms
1 onion, chopped
4 chicken breasts
7 oz (200g) collar bacon, cooked and diced
pinch nutmeg and cayenne pepper

Poach the chicken breasts in the stock. Remove and slice. Sweat the onions and the mushrooms in a pan with 3½ oz (100g) of butter and 3½ oz (100g) flour. Stir with a whisk utilizing the figure 8 method to avoid lumping. Add the chicken stock, bring to a boil and cook for 15 minutes. Then add the bacon and the cream. Check seasonings. When the mixture is cold, spread some of it on the cooked crêpes. Add some sliced chicken and roll. Put the crêpes on a greaseproof baking tray. Sprinkle with grated cheese and bake until hot.

Oliver Queva & Anne Marie Galvin

Max's Wine Bar

BRUNCH CRÊPES

16 entrée crêpes
¼ lb (115g) bulk pork sausage (such as Rosscarbery)
¾ cup chopped onion
2 cloves garlic, minced
1 10 oz (280g) pkg frozen chopped spinach, thawed and
  squeezed free of all liquid
1 egg, beaten
1 cup small curd cottage cheese
¼ cup Parmesan cheese
1 Tbsp parsley flakes
1 teas salt
½ teas each, thyme and marjoram
¼ cup butter or margarine
1 28 oz can (750g) chopped tomatoes, drained
½ teas basil
½ teas salt

Brown sausage in skillet. Remove and drain well. In a little olive oil, sauté onion and garlic until limp. Remove from skillet and drain. Combine sausage, onion, garlic, spinach, egg, cottage cheese, Parmesan cheese, parsley, salt, thyme and marjoram. Mix well. Divide evenly among crêpes and roll up. Place in a single layer in greased shallow baking dish. Dish can be covered and refrigerated at this point. Before serving, make sauce by combining butter, tomatoes, basil, salt and pepper in a saucepan and bringing to a boil. Simmer for 10 minutes. Pour sauce over filled crêpes and bake, uncovered, at 180C/350F for 15 to 20 minutes or until hot.

Jane Bergin

BEEF, LAMB & PORK

Charles Fort

KENYAN TOWER of FILLET of BEEF

For the Tower
6 2oz (50g) escalopes of fillet beef
3 oz (75g) sliced oyster mushrooms
3 oz (75g) beansprouts
3 oz (75g) mangetout
3 oz (75g) sliced capsicums
2 Tbsp (30ml) oriental oyster sauce
2 Tbsp (30ml) light soy sauce
2 Tbsp (30ml) sesame seed oil
1 medium potato

For the Sauce
1 cup brown sugar
1 cup (250ml) vinegar
2 cups (1 lb) chopped tomato
4 teas (20ml) Worcestershire sauce
1 teas (5ml) tomato purée
1 cup (250ml) mango chutney

Starting with the sauce; reduce the sugar and vinegar by ½ in a thick bottom pan. Add the remainder of the sauce ingredients and simmer for 5 minutes. Set aside and keep warm.

Wash and grate the potato, cover in cold water and set to one side.

Stir fry the vegetables quickly and finish with the oyster and soy sauces, and the sesame seed oil. Set aside and keep warm.

Season and grill the escalopes of fillet of beef to taste.

On a heated plate, layer upwards for three layers. Then stir fry vegetables and the escalopes, beginning with the vegetables and finishing with the beef.

Flash fry the potato and drain. Surround the fillet tower with the sauce and sprinkle the top of the tower with the potato and perhaps some cress. Enjoy. **Serves 2.**

Tip: You may use a cocktail stick to hold your tower straight until you get used to stacking them. Just please remember to remove it before eating!

Patrick Bennett
Hurley's Bar & Restaurant

ROAST RACK of LAMB
with LAVENDER SAUCE

Rack of lamb
¼ pint (150ml) white wine
½ pint (300ml) lamb stock
2 oz (55g) butter
glass of dried lavender flowers
1 tomato, diced
Dijon mustard
Breadcrumbs

Preheat oven to 200C/400F. Pan fry the seasoned rack of lamb for 2 to 3 minutes in a small amount of oil. Put in oven and cook as required, approximately 25 minutes for pink lamb.

To make the Sauce: Simmer the white wine and the lamb stock together with the butter. Boil and take off the heat. Add a glass of the dried lavender flowers and leave to infuse. Do not boil as the sauce will then become bitter. Leave as required, the longer the stronger. Then, pass the sauce through a sieve and add the diced tomato.

When the rack is cooked, spread with Dijon mustard and dip in breadcrumbs. Put under the grill until brown. When the rack comes out of the oven, leave it to sit for a couple of minutes and it will finish cooking for itself.

Oliver Queva & Anne Marie Galvin
Max's Wine Bar

54

STUFFED PORK
with PRUNES & APPLES

4 pork chops, 7-8 oz each
4 Granny Smith apples
7 oz (200g) prunes, soaked overnight in water and chopped
4 fl oz (125ml) brandy
4 oz (115g) butter
4 fl oz (125ml) white wine
4 fl oz (125ml) beef stock

Peel, core and chop 2 apples and put them in a saucepan with a little bit of water and 1 oz of butter. When they are cooked, mash the mix, add the prunes and mix together.

Using a long bladed knife, from the smaller side of the pork chop separate in half without cutting all the way through. Place the stuffing inside and close again with a wooden skewer. Pan fry the chops with 1 oz (25g) butter for seven minutes per side. When cooked, flambé with the brandy. Remove the chops from the pan and keep warm. To the pan, add the white wine. Let it reduce, then add the beef stock and the remaining ounce of butter. Whisk the sauce lightly and add brandy if required.

Sauté Apples: Peel and core the remaining 2 apples and cut them into segments. Lightly sauté in 1 oz of butter until brown and caramelized. To serve, cut the chop in half so you can see the stuffing. Arrange the sautéed apples around and pour the sauce over.

Oliver Qveva & Anne Marie Galvin

Max's Wine Bar

RACK of PORK
with BLACK PEPPER & ORANGE

3½-4 lbs (1½-2kgs) rack of pork, chin bone removed
2 Tbls black peppercorns, coarsely crushed
2-3 cloves garlic, crushed
Grated rind and juice of 1 orange
2 teas fresh thyme, chopped
1 Tbls (15ml) olive oil
2-3 shallots or 1 onion, cut into quarters
1 Tbls (15ml) honey

One day ahead, if possible, mix the black pepper, garlic, orange rind, thyme and olive oil together. Press the pepper mixture on to the fat surface. Cover and refrigerate overnight.

Preheat oven 180C/350F. Place the joint on a roasting tin with the shallot or onion and orange juice and a little water and cook or 1½-2 hours. Top up the water during cooking. Don't allow the topping to burn. Cover with foil if necessary. For the last half hour, remove the foil and pour on the honey. When the pork is cooked, wrap in foil. Allow to rest for 20 minutes. Remove the onion from the pan and boil up the juices. Add some wine or water and a knob of butter and serve with the sliced pork.
Serves 6-8.

Barry's Meats

ROAST PORK
with HERBS & GARLIC

3 lbs (1½) loin of pork, boned and trimmed
6-8 Tbls mixed fresh herbs, chopped
    (fennel is especially good with pork)
2-3 cloves garlic, chopped
salt and black pepper
2-3 Tbls (30-45ml) olive oil
Grated rind of one lemon
½ pint (300ml) white wine/water/cider
2 Tbls (30ml) honey

Start a day ahead to allow the pork to marinate and the flavours to mingle. Lay the joint on a large board fat side down. Whiz the herbs, garlic, seasoning, oil and lemon rind in the processor. Spoon half the mixture along the length of the joint and tie it up. Place in the fridge overnight. Keep remaining herb mixture covered in a small bowl also in the fridge.

Preheat oven 180C/350F. Place the joint on a roasting tin, season well, add a few chopped onions, garlic or shallots to flavour the gravy. Add a little water, wine or cider. Cook for 30-35 minutes per lb (1/2kg). Top up with water/wine/cider as necessary.

Forty minutes before end of cooking time spread with honey. When the meat is cooked, wrap in foil. Allow to rest for 20 minutes. Discard the onion, etc. Boil up the juices. Add more liquid, stir up and gather the juices. Season and whisk in a knob of butter. Serve with the thinly sliced pork and a small spoonful of the remaining herb mixture, mixed with a little more olive oil if necessary.
Serves 6.

Barry's Meats

ITALIAN SAUSAGE

2½ lb (1.5kg) boneless pork butt or shoulder, minced
1½ teas dried coriander seeds
1½ teas dried parsley flakes
1 Tbsp fennel seeds
1 large clove garlic, minced
¾ teas salt
¾ teas coarse ground black pepper

With a mortar and pestle or blender, grind the coriander, parsley and fennel into small particles. Add to chopped meat. Add garlic, salt and pepper. Mix well with your hands to distribute seasonings. Cover and refrigerate for at least 8 hours to blend flavours.

For hot spice sausage, add 1 teas (5ml) chili powder or ¼ teas (1 ml) cayenne with the other seasonings.

Bob Hayden

CHILI BEEF CASSEROLE

3 Tbls (75ml) extra virgin olive oil
chopped red onions
mixed varieties of mushrooms
2 lbs (900g) round steak, diced
1 Tbls Vitam Vegetarian Yeast Stock
15 oz (425ml) water
8-16oz (2-300ml) tomato purée
chopped peppers, courgettes and aubergine to suit
1 stalk celery
bay leaf
3-4 chili peppers, chopped to taste
half a bottle red wine
salt and pepper

Gently fry onions and mushrooms in a pot for 5 minutes or so. In a frying pan, add oil and diced round steak and heat until brown. Add the Vitam. Into main pot, add about 15 small new potatoes and the browned diced steak. Pour in the tomato purée. Add the rest of the ingredients. Gently heat, avoid boiling, stirring occasionally until the potatoes are ready. Remove bay leaf. Serve.

James McKeown
The Sovereign House

STUFFED ROUND STEAK

2 lbs (900g) round steak (one piece)
1 pint (600ml) beef stock (Oxo/Knorr cube will suffice)

Stuffing
2 cups (450g) bread crumbs
small onion, chopped
2 teas parsley, chopped
1 teas thyme, chopped
salt and pepper

Preheat oven 160C/300F. Mix all the stuffing ingredients together. Trim the steak and flatten with a rolling pin. Place the stuffing at one end of the steak and roll up. Use skewers to secure. Brown on all sides in hot fat. Place in an oven-proof dish and pour stock around it. Cook for 2½ hours.

Note: Sliced mushrooms may be added to the stuffing if desired.

Bride Acton

MURPHY'S BEEF

3 Tbsp (45ml) oil
1 lb 9oz (700g) chuck steak, cut into ½ inch cubes
2 large onions, sliced
2 cloves garlic, minced
1 Tbsp dark brown sugar
1 Tbsp flour
10 fl oz (300ml) stout (Murphys!)
½ pint (300ml) beef stock
2 bay leaves and 2 sprigs thyme
8 oz (225g) mixed mushrooms, sliced
1 oz (25g) butter

Croûtes
1 small baguette, sliced
2 teas (10ml) wholegrain mustard
1 oz (25g) butter, softened

Preheat oven to 150C/300F. Heat 1 Tbsp (15ml) oil in a frying pan. Brown meat in batches and transfer to a casserole dish. Add remaining oil to the pan and cook onions until soft. Stir in garlic and sugar, cook for 1 minute. Add flour, stout and stock; bring to the boil, season and put in casserole. Add bay leaves and thyme, cover and cook for 1½ hours. Half an hour before beef is ready, sauté mushrooms in butter and add to meat.

To Make croûtes: Toast baguette on one side. Mix together the mustard and butter, spread on untoasted side and grill until golden and crispy. Serve beef with rice, croûtes and fresh thyme.

Serves 4.

Anne Fitzsimons

VEAL STEAK
on a TRUFFLE RISOTTO
with LEMON SCENTED
PAN JUICES

2½ lbs (1 kg) loin of veal, cut into 4 steaks
½ lemon
olive oil

Risotto
7 oz (200g) aborio rice
1 pint (600g) chicken stock
1 shallot
1 small clove garlic
1½ (40g) butter
¾ oz (20g) Parmesan cheese
truffles (white, preferable from Alba in Italy)

Finely chop the shallot and garlic. Gently fry in a little butter until glossy. Add rice and continue frying until rice becomes glossy also. Add chicken stock and simmer very gently for 20 minutes, stirring constantly. While the rice is cooking, heat a pan and fry the veal steaks, very hot at first, then reducing the heat. When the veal is medium done, remove from the heat and allow to rest until the rice is cooked. When the rice is ¾ cooked, add the remaining butter and Parmesan cheese. Cook fully, then remove from heat. Add truffles, very finely grated and season. Serve the risotto in the centre of the plate with veal steak presented on top. For the veal sauce, squeeze the half lemon into the pan juices and reduce to sauce consistency.

Urban & Jackie Mutter
Old Head Golf Link Restaurant

LAMB STEW

½ lb diced lamb
4 carrots, sliced
3 stalks celery, sliced
2 parsnips, sliced
2 onions, chopped
8 potatoes, chopped
2 vegetable stock cubes
2 teas chopped herbs
2 Tbsp (30ml) olive oil

Heat oil in a pan. Add lamb and chopped herbs and cook for 15 minutes. Transfer lamb to a large pot. Sauté carrots, celery, onions, and parsnips in olive oil for 10 minutes. Add to lamb together with 2 pints of vegetable stock and cook for 40 minutes. Then add the potatoes and cook for 15-20 minutes longer. Mix a little cornflour (cornstarch) with water and stir into the stew. Simmer for another few minutes and serve.

Mary Lane
Mary Lane's Biftro

POULTRY & GAME

Casey's Corner

EASY CHICKEN DISH

1 clove garlic
1 large onion
½ lb (115g) mushrooms
2 chicken breasts
2 chicken Oxo cubes
1 small carton cream
a little brandy, optional
oil for cooking

Chop garlic, onion and mushrooms. Add oil to pan and cook them until they soften. Slice chicken into small pieces. Add to pan and cook until chicken is cooked through. Add cream (and brandy), and stir through the mixture. Simmer for about five minutes, then add Oxo cubes. Mix well.

Note: This dish can be made the day before or early in the day and can be reheated and served on a bed of rice, or with potatoes and vegetables.

Eileen O'Connell

MARINATED BREAST of CHICKEN in GUINNESS and SPICES with ROASTED VEGETABLES

4 breasts of chicken
   with skin if possible
2 carrots
1 red pepper
1 green pepper
1 yellow pepper
½ head cauliflower
4 cloves garlic
olive oil

Marinade:

2 pints Guinness
½ teas ground nutmeg
½ teas ground ginger
½ teas ground cinnamon
2 Tbsp brown sugar
2 Tbsp (30ml) honey

Place all the ingredients for the marinade into a pot and reduce down by half. Let the mixture cool down and pour over the chicken. Then place it in the fridge overnight.

Peel the carrots and cut into 2½"long pieces. Clean the peppers and cut them in quarters; cut the cauliflower into small pieces. Place the vegetables in a roasting tray and coat them with olive oil and seasoning. Cook them, together with the crushed garlic in a high oven (200C/450F) until golden brown. Strain the chicken from the marinade and panfry over a low heat to prevent the chicken going black.

For the Sauce just reduce the marinade until a smooth texture (syrup), then season. Place your vegetables in the middle of a plate and the chicken on top with the sauce around. Garnish with herbs.

Blue Haven

CHICKEN CURRY

1 cooked chicken
2 oz (55g) butter
2 cloves garlic
1 large onion
5 medium mushrooms
4 teas mild curry powder
4 teas flour
1 Knorr chicken stock cube
half pint (300ml) water
2 Tbsp (30ml) mango chutney
salt and pepper
apple, sultanas
packet of boil in the bag white or brown rice

Melt the butter in a large pan, add chopped garlic, mushrooms, and onion. Allow to cook gently for a few minutes. Add curry powder and flour; mix well. Add stock cube and cold water. Simmer for 15 minutes, then add mango chutney. Add pieces of cooked chicken and seasoning. While the curry is simmering, into another pot, pour 2 pints of boiling water; add salt and rice and cook for 15-20 minutes. Before serving the curry, add chopped apple and sultanas. Serve on a bed of rice.
Serves 4.

Anne Doyle

CHICKEN
with MUSHROOM SAUCE

2 chicken breasts
2 rashers of bacon
2 oz (55g) breadcrumbs
2 oz (55g) mature Cheddar
2 oz (55g) butter
6 spring onions
4 fl oz (125ml) chicken stock
4 fl oz (125ml) white wine
4 oz (115g) mushrooms
7 oz container (200ml) sour cream
black pepper

Slice chicken breasts. Divide cheese between 2 chicken breasts. Cover with sour cream and roll in a rasher. Roll in breadcrumbs. Turn quickly in hot butter. Cook in oven at 200C/400F for 45 minutes. Meanwhile, add stock to butter in pan. Add wine and mushrooms. Reduce by ¾. Add the sour cream, chopped spring onions and pepper. Add to chicken for last ¼ hour.

Sheila Ryan

POULET AUGEÉ

1 chicken, boned and chopped into cubes
1 lb green or smoked bacon, cut into cubes and boiled for 10
mins
4 courgettes, chopped
2 large carrots
¼ lb (115g) mushrooms
1 green and red pepper
garlic to taste
2 fl oz (50ml) cream

Season the chicken and cook at a high heat in heavy saucepan with virgin olive oil for 5-10 minutes until golden. Add bacon and the chopped vegetables and leave to simmer for 45 minutes in a tightly sealed pot. Add cream at the end. Serve with a green salad or rice.

Pacelli Nolan

CURRY CHEZ GLEÁNN RADHARE

In a cup, mix together:
2 teas turmeric
2 teas chili powder
2 teas coriander
1 teas ground ginger
1 teas cumin
1 teas paprika

8 oz (225g) mushrooms, quartered
2 medium onions, chopped
6 cloves garlic, chopped
half a tin coconut milk
half a tin chopped tomatoes
1 cup (250ml) red wine
8 oz (225ml) chicken stock (use 2 cubes)
4 chicken fillets, cut into bite size pieces
olive oil

Sweat onions and garlic in olive oil in a wok and put aside in a dish. Seal bite-size chicken pieces in wok and put aside in a dish. Put a little oil in wok and fry spices; then add some chicken stock to make a paste. Cook slowly for 4 minutes, then add rest of the chicken stock. Bring to the boil and add everything else. Simmer for 20 minutes and serve over rice.

Bob White

MARINATED BREASTS of WILD PIGEON with STAUTONS WHITE PUDDING ROAST GARLIC & WILD MUSHROOM COMPOTE

Source some wild pigeon if you know a hunter, or purchase from a good butcher; use the legs for stock. Bone out the breasts of pigeon; 2-3 are ample for a starter. Using the legs and breastbone, some carrots, leeks, celery, onions, red wine and a pint of water, make a stock and simmer for 1½ hours. Strain and reduce the liquid by half. This you will use as your sauce.

To make the Compote: Peel 4 cloves of garlic and gently roast in some olive oil. While they are roasting, peel the onion, chop and sweat off in some butter. Add your wild mushrooms, as many varieties as possible but if you only have one, it will do. Now get 4 oz of white pudding; peel the skin off and chop it up. Add your garlic to the onion and wild mushroom mixture. To the pot, add a little whiskey or brandy, whichever takes your fancy. Now add the pudding. This will bring the whole lot together. Now, panfry your pigeon. I generally like to serve it rare or pink, but cook it to your own taste. When ready, place on a plate with a little of the heaped compote. Then add some stock to your pan. Reduce a little and pour over the pigeon.

Mark Russell
The White House

GINGER CHICKEN

4 chicken fillets
¼ pint (150ml) cream
1 Tbsp fresh ginger
1 Tbsp (15ml) honey
pinch of chopped herbs
1 Tbsp (15ml) olive oil
1 orange

Heat the oil in a pan. Add chopped herbs. Cook chicken fillets for 15-20 minutes, turning regularly until cooked. Using another small pan, heat the cream to boiling. Add the honey and ginger and simmer for 3 minutes on low heat. To serve, arrange the chicken on a plate and cover with sauce. Garnish with a side salad and sliced orange. Serve with boiled rice.

Mary Lane
Mary Lane's Bistro

SEARED BREAST of DUCK COATED with a HONEY & BLACK PEPPER CORN CRUST

VANILLA & SWEET POTATO BREAD PUDDING

SALAD of MIXED BEANS

VEGETABLE SPRING ROLL served with a CONTREAU & BLACKBERRY SYRUP

Crusted Breasts Duck:

2 breasts of Barbary duck
cracked black pepper
4 Tbsp (60ml) honey

Sweet Potato bread pudding:

2 vanilla pods
½ pint (300ml) milk
4 egg yolks
1 sweet potato
4 slices of white bread

Salad:

4 oz (115g) mixed beans

Spring Roll:

1 carrot, fine julienne
1 parsnip, fine julienne
1 courgette, fine julienne
2 sheets of filo pastry

Sauce:

4 oz (115g) castor sugar
3 fl oz (85ml) vinegar
Contreau
blackberry juice
whole blackberries

To make the custard: Heat the milk in a saucepan to 38 degrees. Pour over the beaten eggs and replace back into a clean saucepan. Cook gently until slightly thickened. Allow to cool. For the spring roll, peel the carrot, parsnip, courgette and cut them into fine strips. Cook until soft in a small saucepan. Cool and wrap in the filo pastry, not forgetting to season with a little salt and pepper.

Cook the mixed beans for about a half hour, or until the beans are soft. Cool. Cook the sweet potato and mash it. Add to the custard. Pour over the slices of bread and allow to soak. Bake in a moderate oven until firm.

To make the sauce: Place the sugar and vinegar in a saucepan and carmalize. Add the contreau and blackberry juice.

To prepare the duck: Sear the duck breasts on a hot pan until golden brown on the skin side Brush with honey and roll in black peppercorns. Place back on the pan to finish the cooking. Finally, assemble the dish by carving the duck. Place on top of the beans with a slice of bread pudding, the spring roll and finish with the sauce. Garnish with a few fresh blackberries.

Paul McBride

Winner Several Gold Medals
Actors

75

Seafood

the Marina

MONKFISH CARPACCIO
with LEMON JUICE & OLIVE OIL

3½ oz (100g) monkfish (fresh & trimmed free of skin &
bone)
¾ oz (20ml) olive oil
¾ oz (20ml) lemon juice
salt and pepper
cherry tomato and chives to garnish

Slice monkfish as thin as possible. Then place between two
sheets of clear plastic and gently, with the palm of the hand,
flatten until paper thin. Brush the base of the plate with olive
oil and cover with monkfish. Place lemon juice in a round
bowl. Season with salt and pepper and slowly whisk in
remaining olive oil. Brush the monkfish with lemon olive oil.
Garnish with a cherry tomato and chives and serve.
One portion.

Urban & Jackie Mutter
Old Head Golf Link Restaurant

THE SPINNAKER'S SPECIAL

1½ lb (700g) grilled fillet of cod on a bed of minted, mushy peas and served with a cream of vermouth sauce.

Sauce:
½ pint (300ml) fish stock
add ½ glass Martini (dry) sweet white wine Sauvignon
Reduce then add salt and pepper and fresh cream

Grill the cod for 2 minutes on each side. Put in a roasting tray and bake for 8-10 minutes, depending on the size of the fish. Cook mushy peas in water; add butter, fresh mint, black pepper and sea salt.

Frank O'Flynn

The Spinnaker

SALMON STEAKS
with MUSCADET, WATERCRESS
& DILL POTATOES

The flavours of the salmon, wine and watercress blend together to create a light and refreshing main course.

1½ lb (625g) waxy potatoes, such as Pink Fir Apple, French
    Ratte, Maris Piper or Wilja
small bunch of fresh dill
3 oz (85g) butter
4 7ox (200g) salmon steaks
2 fl oz (50ml) Muscadet or other dry white wine
1 Tbsp (15ml) virgin olive oil
½ teas (2.5ml) white wine vinegar
3 oz (85g) watercress
4 fl oz (125ml) fish stock chicken stock or water
1 Tbsp roughly chopped fresh parsley
seasoning

1. Prepare the potatoes. If you are using Pink Fir Apple, remove any knobs before peeling (Pink Fir apple and French Ratte need not be peeled thoroughly, so don't worry about doing a perfect job). If using Wilja or any other large potatoes, cut them in half lengthways; then, with the cut sides facing upwards, halve them lengthways again to make thick wedges. Simmer the potatoes in boiling, salted water with most of the dill. Reserve the remaining dill for the garnish.

2. Clarify 1oz (25g) of the butter by melting it in a very small pan over a high heat. The butter will melt and bubble fiercely when its water content begins to boil. When the bubbling subsides, remove the pan from the heat and leave for about a minute until the solids have settled on the bottom of the pan.

Pour the clear, clarified butter into an ovenproof frying pan, large enough to take the four salmon steaks.

3. Preheat the oven to 190C/375F/Gas5. Heat the clarified butter in the frying pan, then add some seasoning. Add the salmon and brown on both sides over a high heat for 2 minutes. Remove from the heat and leave to stand for 30 seconds. Pour the wine over the salmon, then bake in the oven for about 5 minutes. Remove from the oven and test to see if the fish is cooked. When it is ready, remove from the pan and keep warm. Do not wash the pan.

4. Combine the oil and vinegar in a bowl with half a teaspoon of salt. Toss the watercress in the dressing until it is thinly coated.

5. Pour the stock or water into the pan in which the fish was cooked, bring to the boil and add the remaining butter. Boil until reduced by half. Pass the sauce through a fine sieve into a pan, add the parsley and reheat briefly.

6. Drain the potatoes. Place the salmon steaks on warmed serving plates, sprikling the reserved dill over the potatoes. Pour the sauce over the fish and serve.
Serves 4.

Note: For fan ovens, preheat the oven to 170C/325F for 5 minutes, then cook for 5 minutes.

Sheila Cullen

ESCALOPE of SALMON
with WATERCRESS SAUCE

2¼ lb (1kg) middle-cut salmon
sea salt
2 oz (55g) clarified butter
½ pint (300ml) fish stock
12 oz (350g) watercress, stalks removed
½ pint (300ml) double cream

Ask your fishmonger to bone out the salmon from the back and remove the skin. Cut the salmon into 4 good slices, lay them on a tea towel and sprinkle lightly with salt. Heat the clarified butter in a sauté pan over moderate heat. Put in the salmon and cook for 5 minutes on each side, then remove from the pan and keep warm. Pour off the fat from the pan and add the fish stock to the pan, scraping to remove any sediment. As soon as the liquid bubbles, toss in the watercress leaves and simmer for 2 minutes, then add the cream. Bring to the boil, then reduce the heat, cover the pan and cook gently for 5 minutes. Adjust the seasoning, the divide the sauce between 4 warmed plates and lay the salmon on top. Garnish with fresh watercress and serve immediately with new potatoes.
Serves 4.

Finder's Inn Restaurant

CHEESE & TOMATO BAKED HADDOCK

4 oz (115g) full-fat soft cheese such as Philadelphia
2 Tbsp (30ml) of milk
2 Tbsp of freshly chopped parsley or coriander
2 8 ox (225g) thick pieces smoked haddock fillet
2 tomatoes, thinly sliced
2 oz (55g) Cheddar or mozzarella cheese, grated
sea salt flakes to sprinkle on top

Preheat the over to 200C/400F. Grease a shallow baking tray. In a bowl, mix together the full-fat soft cheese, milk and coriander or parsley until smooth. Season with salt and freshly ground black pepper. Place the haddock fillets, skin side down, on the baking tray. Spread the soft cheese mixture over the top. Place the tomato slices on the soft cheese, then sprinkle the Cheddar or mozzarella over the top followed by salt flakes and ground black pepper. Bake for 20 minutes until the fish flakes easily and the cheese is melted, bubbling and golden. Serve immediately.
Serves 2.

Jill Barry

DUBLIN LAWYER

1 fresh lobster
5 oz (150ml) fresh cream
2 oz (55g) butter
4 Tbsp (60ml) Irish whiskey
salt and pepper

Kill the lobster by plunging a sharp instrument into the cross on the head. Cut it in two lengthwise. Remove the meat from the tail and claws of the lobster but keep the shell. Cut the meat into chunks. Heat the butter but do not let it brown. Add the raw lobster meat. Season to taste. Pour the warmed Irish whiskey over it and flame. Mix the cream with the pan juices and gently heat but do not boil. Replace the lobster meat in the half shells. Pour the sauce over and serve hot.

Philip McEvoy
The Old Presbytery
Luxury B & B

TRI-COLOURED HADDOCK

3 lb (1.3kg) haddock
1 Tbsp (15ml) oil
6 oz (175g) rice
1 ¼ pints (700ml) water
½ teas salt
1 Tbsp (15ml) lemon juice
2 oz (55g) butter
2 oz (55g) sultanas
1 diced apple
1 diced onion
2 tear curry powder
2 teas cornflour (cornstarch)
8 oz (225ml) stock
8 oz (225ml) cream

Clean haddock, remove eyes, brush all over with oil and bake for 25 minutes at 190C/375F. Boil rice in water, salt and lemon juice.

Sauce: Put butter, sultanas, apple, onion, curry powder, salt and pepper in saucepan and cook for 45 minutes. Add stock, bring to boil, mix in cornflour and remove from heat. Add in cream, do not put back on heat. Place fish on heated serving dish, spoon rice around the edge; next pour sauce around fish. Garnish with olives, fennel, lemon, cucumber and tomato.

Elizabeth Harrington

FILLET of SOLE PALM BEACH

2 fillet of sole
2 bananas
1 egg
1 lemon
1 oz (25g) butter
flour
breadcrumbs
Worcestershire sauce
Flaked almonds
Salt & pepper
Parsley

Peel the bananas and roll a fillet of sole around each one. Season with salt and pepper, lemon juice and Worcestershire sauce. Roll in flour, egg wash and breadcrumbs. Fry in deep fat fryer. Fry flaked almonds in butter until golden brown and serve over the sole garnished with lemon and parsley. Serve with rice and curry sauce.

Manfred Schick

PAUPIETTE'S of JOHN DORY with WILD BABY NETTLES and SMOKED SALMON

3 medium fillets of John Dory (skinned & boned)
3 small slices of smoked salmon
3 oz (75g) blanched, diced young nettle leaves
3 oz (75g) cherry tomatoes
½ oz (15g) unsalted butter
1 cup (250ml) white wine
½ cup (125ml) double cream
juice of ¼ lemon
1 sprig of fresh dill or fennel

Spread out fillets, skin side downwards. Layer the salmon on top of the fillets and on top of these place the nettles. Roll John Dory fillets, salmon and nettles from the head end to the tail end and secure with cocktail sticks. Place in a pan with the tomato, butter, wine and lemon juice. Gently poach for 5 minutes. Add the cream and simmer for 1 minute. Serve on a warm plate using the herb as a simple garnish. **One portion.** Bon appétit.

Patrick Bennett
Hurley's Bar & Restaurant

GRILLED KING PRAWNS

6 whole fresh king prawns
clove garlic
lemon
salt
olive oil
2 oz (55g) butter

Coat prawns in oil. Place on grill. Smother with butter and garlic. Season with salt and lemon. Grill for 4 approximately 4 minutes. Serve with garlic butter. Garnish with lemon wedges.

Bob Carpenter

Annelie's

SOLE STUFFED
with SEAFOOD

1 fillet of large sole
3 prawns, shelled
3 crab claws
2 oz (55g) fresh salmon
2 oz (55g) smoked haddock
2 mussels
2 oz (55g) margarine & 2 oz (55g) flour for roux
lemon
salt
4 teas (30ml) cream
Cheddar cheese

Place all fish excluding the sole in boiling water with lemon and salt. Return to boil, then remove all fish. Add half of the roux to the fish stock and thicken to your own liking. Add cream and simmer for a few minutes.

Prepare sole: Dip in flour and skewer to hold shape. Season with lemon and salt. Put into deep fryer and cook until golden brown. Remove skewer and place sole on a serving platter, seafood in centre. Pour sauce over seafood, top with cheese and place under grill until cheese melts. Serve with new potatoes, French beans and lemon wedges.

Bob Carpenter

Annelie's

HALIBUT
with ORANGE & HORSERADISH CRUST

10 oz (280g) dry breadcrumbs
5 oz (140g) horseradish, finely grated
3 oz (85g) orange peel, finely grated
4 cloves garlic, chopped
12 6 oz (175g) halibut steaks
salt and pepper
1 cup (250ml) olive oil
1 cup (250ml) herbed olive oil
4 oz (115g) orange segments

Combine crumbs, horseradish, orange zest and garlic. Bread
the halibut previously seasoned. Pan fry in oil. Finish the
fish in a 190C/375F oven. Garnish with herbed olive oil and
orange segments.
Serves 3.

Shane McClements

Kierns Folkhouse Kinsale

PLAICE FILLETS

4 plaice fillets
butter or olive oil
garlic
fennel
2 tomatoes
4 Tbsp (60ml) Irish whiskey
cream

Fry the fillets in butter or olive oil. Keep warm. In saucepan, crush a garlic clove, fennel cut in strips and tomatoes finely sliced. Add ¼ cup (60ml) of whiskey and the same of cream. Heat through. Pour over fish and serve.
Serves 4.

Mrs. Barbara Matson

RAY WINGS in CAPER BUTTER

A simple but tasty favourite in our restaurant.

1 large fresh ray wing
½ cup (115g) flour
salt and pepper
1 Tbsp capers

Using a large frying pan, add oil and teaspoon of butter. Heat until hot. Dust ray wing in flour seasoned with salt and pepper. Put a tablespoon of capers in the centre of a hot pan and immediately press ray wing onto capers. Leave on high for 3-4 minutes. Turn over and leave on high for 2 minutes. Turn down to simmer, cover with lid and cook for a further 5 minutes. Serve with minted new potatoes and fresh garden peas, or other seasonal vegetables and lemon wedges.

Richard Ennos
Little Skillet

WARM SALAD
of CHILI SEAFOOD

Mix of lettuces (oak leaf, lollorossa, iceberg and frisse)
Pickled cucumber (finely sliced cucumber marinated for 2
  hours with equal portions of white vinegar and sugar)
2 diced tomatoes
4 oz (115g) diced salmon
6 oz (175g) diced white fish (monkfish, red gurnard, squid or
John Dory)
4 whole prawns
8 mussels in the shell
2-3 oz (65-85g) chickpeas
4 Tbsp (60ml) sweet chili sauce
1 Tbsp chopped garlic
2 Tbsp pesto
juice of 1 lemon

In a large frying pan, heat a bit of olive oil. Add fish and sauté
for 2-3 minutes. Then add the chickpeas, chili sauce, garlic,
pesto and the lemon. Cook for 1 more minute. To serve,
arrange the seafood artistically on top of the salad. Garnish
with parsnip chips. **Serves 4.**

Parsnip Chips: Deep fry finely sliced parsnips in sunflower oil
until golden brown. Cool and season with salt. Sprinkle with
toasted sesame seeds.

Martin Shanahan
Kinsale Gourmet Store
Listed in the
100 BEST RESTAURANTS IN IRELAND 2000

TEATIME

Newman's Mall

DEVILED HAM TOASTS

2 oz (55g) lean ham, finely chopped
2 teas (10ml) Worcestershire sauce
cayenne pepper
2 teas French mustard
½ oz chopped fresh parsley

Cut a circle from each slice of toast with a sharp knife, using a biscuit cutter or a teacup as the template. Amalgamate the ham, Worcestershire sauce, cayenne and French mustard. Melt the butter in a small pan and stir in the mixture. Heat until it starts to sizzle, then pile it onto the toast circles. Crown with parsley and serve immediately.

Louise Hayes

DAINTY TEA TIME SANDWICHES

1 3 oz (85g) package cream cheese, softened
1 Tbsp (15ml) cream
2 teas finely chopped chives
6 thin slices sandwich bread
½ English cucumber, unpeeled and thinly sliced
½ cup (4oz) finely minced parsley

In a small bowl, mix the cream cheese with the cream and chives; set aside.

Using a 2 inch (5cm) round cookie cutter, cut 2 circles from each slice of bread. Spread the cream cheese mixture lightly on each circle. Top each with a slice of cucumber. Sprinkle with the finely chopped parsley. Arrange on a serving plate. Cover lightly with wax paper and refrigerate until serving time. **Yield: 12 tea sandwiches.**

Anonymous

BOILED FRUIT CAKE

1 lb (450g) sultanas or raisins
½ lb (225g) butter or margarine
7 oz (200g) sugar
10 oz (280g) flour
½ teas ground cloves
½ teas nutmeg
½ teas salt
½ teas mixed spice
¼ teas bread soda (baking soda)
2 eggs
1 cup (250ml) water

Boil prepared fruit, sugar, butter and water together for 10 minutes. Allow to cool. Stir well while cooking. Then add the flour and spices together with the bread soda and salt. Fold in the eggs which have been beaten first. Turn into a greased 7 inch square tin. Bake in a moderate oven 150C/300F for 1½-2 hours. Turn out and cool on a wire rack.

Joyce O'Brien

BOILED FRUIT CAKE II

1 lb (450g) dried fruit (sultanas, raisins, currants)
6 oz (175g) mixed peel
4 oz (115g) cherries
½ lb (225g) butter
3 eggs
12 oz (350g) brown sugar
12 oz (350g) plain flour
1 teas baking powder
Mixed spice
Pinch of salt
Small drop of whiskey

Place fruit in a saucepan, cover with water and simmer gently for 5 minutes. Strain off water and return the hot fruit to the saucepan. Chop the butter and place on top of the fruit, add the sugar and mix until the butter melts. Beat in the eggs. Stir in flour, baking powder, spice and pinch of salt. Add a small drop of whiskey. Bake for about 2 hours at 170C/325F.

Bride Acton

SPECIAL SCONES

2¾ cups all purpose flour
6 Tbsp sugar
1½ tbsp baking powder
1 teas salt
½ cup chilled, unsalted butter, diced
¾ cup chocolate chips or raisins
1 cup chilled whipping cream
2 large eggs

Preheat oven to 200C/400F. Lightly dust baking sheet with flour. Sift first 4 ingredients into large bowl. Add butter and blend with fingertips until mixture resembles coarse meal. Mix in the chocolate chips. Whisk cream and eggs in small bowl to blend. Pour over crumb mixture, stirring just until combined.

Transfer dough to lightly floured work surface. Press into 1-inch thick round. Cut out rounds using 3-inch round cookie cutter. Gather dough scraps and press to thickness of 1 inch. Cut out additional rounds. Transfer scones to prepared baking tin and sprinkle with additional sugar. Bake 10 minutes. Reduce oven temperature to 180C/350F and continue baking until light brown, about 18 minutes. Cool slightly. Serve scones warm.

Fiona Fitzgerald

CRANBERRY SCONES

8 oz (225g) self-raising flour
1 level teas baking powder
pinch of salt
3 oz (85g) butter or margarine
1 rounded Tbsp sugar
5 fl oz (150ml) milk
3 oz (85g) dried cranberries
egg

Preheat oven 200C/425F. Sieve flour, baking powder and salt. Rub in the butter. Add sugar and cranberries. Stir in enough milk to give a soft dough and roll out lightly on a floured surface. Cut into rounds, brush with beaten egg and bake until well risen and golden brown, about 12 minutes.

Violet Howe

BANANA SPECIAL

2 bananas, mashed
caster sugar (superfine)
3-4 dessert spoons (21-28ml) natural youghurt
digestive biscuits

Sweeten the bananas with a little sugar and blend together with the youghurt. Layer in a tall glass with the biscuits, starting with the biscuits as a base. Top with ice cream and sliced Kiwi or other fruit.

Jane Coleman

age 12

ALMOND SLICES

½ lb (225g) butter or margarine
½ lb (225g) sugar
¾ lb (350g) self-raising flour
2 teas (30ml) almond essence
2 eggs, beaten
split almonds to decorate

Preheat oven 170C/325F. Melt the margarine and sugar. Add the flour. Stir in the egg and the almond essence. Pour into a baking tin. Decorate with almonds. Bake for approximately 20 minutes. Allow to cool in the tin and cut into slices or squares.

Dominic Lawrence

CHOCOLATE BISCUIT CAKE

2 Tbsp cocoa
3 oz (85g) butter
1 egg, slightly beaten
4 oz (115g) sugar
½ lb (225g) broken biscuits (rich tea)
4 oz (115g) plain chocolate for icing

Melt butter in a saucepan. Add sugar, cocoa and egg. Cook slowly for about 5 minutes. Remove and add the biscuits. Stir well. Line a 7 inch square tin with paper. Pour in mixture. Press well down. Leave to set. Melt chocolate over hot water and pour over cake.

EASY LEMON PUDDING

2 blocks (pints) vanilla ice cream
1 package lemon jelly
2 lemons, grated rind and juice

Grate lemons and squeeze juice. Dissolve jelly in lemon juice over heat. Put ice cream in a large bowl to soften and add the lemon mixture. Beat well together. Put into a serving bowl and sprinkle with lemon/orange rind or milk flake.

Mary Lawrence

LEMON TART

8 medium eggs
10 oz (280g) caster (superfine) sugar
15 oz (450ml) cream
juice of 4 lemons

Preheat oven 150C/300F. Cream together the eggs and the sugar. First add the cream and then the lemon juice. Pour into a 9 inch pastry case baked blind and cook for one hour until set. Boil the zest in sugar syrup for garnish.

CHOCOLATE MARQUISE

6 oz (175g) dark chocolate
1½ Tbsp butter
2 leaves gelatin
3 oz (85g) icing (powdered sugar
4 egg yolks
3 Tbsp cocoa
6 Tbsp (90ml) cream
3 egg whites

Melt the chocolate and butter together. Add gelatin. Whisk sugar and egg yolks until thick. Add sieved Cocoa. Whisk cream until thick. Whisk egg whites until stiff. To the whipped cream, fold in the egg yolk mixture, then the melted chocolate and lastly the egg whites. Pour into a 2lb tin lined with cling film.

Michael Reese
Old Bank House

MILLENNIUM GINGER CAKE

6 oz (175g) plain white flour
1 teas ground ginger
2½ teas cinnamon
1¼ teas mixed spice
pinch of salt
3 oz (85g) butter
3 oz (85g) soft brown sugar
2 Tbsp (30ml) treacle
2 Tbsp (30ml) golden syrup
Grated rind of 1 small orange
1 egg and 5 Tbsp (65ml) milk, blended together
½ teas bread soda (baking soda), dissolved in a little water
2 oz (55g) crystallized ginger

Preheat oven 170C/325F. Sieve together the first 5 ingredients. Melt the next 4 ingredients over low heat. Then allow to cool for 5 minutes. Make a well in the centre of the flour. Add melted ingredients together with the egg/milk and grated orange rind. Beat until the mixture is perfectly smooth. Lastly, add the bicarbonate of soda and mix well. Bake for 1 hour, testing to see if it is done. Allow to stand for 10 minutes before removing from the tin.

Topping: Blend 2 oz (50g) icing (powdered) sugar with a little orange juice. Drizzle over the top and decorate with sliced ginger pieces.

Note: The flavour of this cake improves if stored in an airtight container for a few days.

Violet Howe

MOLLIE'S LEMON BARS

Bottom Layer
1 cup (225g) butter
2 cups (450g) flour
½ cup (115g) icing (powdered) sugar

Mix all together, then pat into a greased 9 X 13 inch pan.
Bake at 170C/325F for 25 minutes.

Top Layer
Meanwhile, beat together 4 eggs and then add the following:
2 cups (450g) sugar
¼ cup (60ml) lemon juice
¼ cup (55g) flour
1 teas baking powder

Mix all together, then pour over hot crust and bake an additional 30 minutes, having increased the oven temperature to
180C/350F. Cool, then sprinkle with icing (powdered) sugar
and enjoy.

Note: *These also freeze well.*

Jane Bergin

RICH FRUIT CAKE

1 lb (450g) plain flour
½ teas salt
1 teas mixed spice
½ teas grated nutmeg
4 oz (115g) ground almonds
12 oz (350g) butter or margarine
12 oz (350g) sugar or soft brown sugar
1 apple, grated
1 orange rind, grated
6 eggs
1 lb (450g) each, sultanas and raisins
8 oz (225g) each, currants and halved cherries
6 oz (175g) chopped dates
6 oz (175g) chopped mixed peel
4 oz (115g) roughly chopped walnuts
15 oz (425g) tin strawberries or apricots
2 Tbsp (30ml) whiskey, brandy or rum
2 Tbsp (30ml) extra spirits, optional
2 teas (10ml) gravy browning, optional

Grease and line a 10 inch/25cm round or a 9 inch/22cm square deep cake tin, using greaseproof or non-stick baking paper. Put all the dried fruit into a large bowl, stoning the dates if necessary. Drain the tinned fruit and discard the juice. Cut up the strawberries or apricots. Add to the dried fruit with the grated orange rind and the grated apple. Stir in the spirits and set aside.

Have the butter or margarine and the eggs at room temperature, and set the oven at 170C/325F. Beat the butter with the
sugar until light and fluffy. Stir in the ground almonds, then
beat in the lightly whisked eggs, a little at a time.

Sieve the flour with the salt and spices and add a spoonful of
flour mixture when the mixture begins to show signs of cur-
dling. Beat in well. Fold in the rest of the flour, stir in the
fruit and nuts, mixing lightly but evenly. Put into the prepared tin or tins and smooth over the top making a slight hollow in the centre. Cook on the middle shelf of the oven for
the first half hour, then lower the temperature to 150C/350F
and continue cooking for 4½ to 5¼ hours for the larger cake
or about 3½ hours for the smaller cake. Check the progress
after the first 1½ hours and place a doubled greaseproof paper
over the top of the lining paper when the cake begins to
brown on top to keep it from darkening too much. Toward
the end of the cooking time, test the cake: press the top of the
cake with a fingertip – it should feel firm. Insert a fine steel
skewer into the centre of the cake and make sure it can be
withdrawn dry. Take from the oven and if desired, prick all
over with the skewer and dribble on the optional 2 Tbsp
(30ml) of spirits. Leave to cool in the tin, then turn out on to
a wire rack. Re-wrap and store until required.

Frosting: The larger cake will need 3 lb (1.30kg) marzipan to
cover the top and sides, half that amount for the top only and
about 2 lb (900g) fondant icing or Royal icing.

Elma O'Donoghue

PASSION CAKE

6 oz (175g) self-raising flour
¼ level teas ground cinnamon
2 level teas baking powder
5 oz (140g) dark brown sugar
2 oz (55g) chopped walnuts
4 oz (115g) carrots, peeled and grated
2 ripe bananas, peeled and mashed
2 eggs
5 oz (150ml) corn oil
½ teas (2.5ml) vanilla essence

Topping:
3 oz (85g) butter, softened
3 oz (85g) package Philadelphia cream cheese, softened
6 oz (175g) icing (powdered) sugar, sieved
½ teas (2.5ml) vanilla essence

Preheat oven 180C/350F.

Mix the flour, cinnamon and baking powder together. Stir in the sugar, walnuts, carrots and bananas. Mix until blended. Make a well in the center; add eggs, oil and vanilla essence. Beat well until blended. Bake in a round 8 inch (20cm) tin for 1¼ hours.

Isabelle Lynch

POCKET CAKE

8 oz (225g) self-raising flour
½ teas cinnamon
½ teas nutmeg
6 oz (175g) butter or margarine
4 oz (115g) light brown sugar
2 oz (55g) mixed peel
6 oz (175g) currants
2 eggs
5 fl oz (150ml) stout

Preheat oven 160C/325F.

Mix the flour, cinnamon and nutmeg together in a bowl. Rub in the butter. Stir in sugar, peel and currants. Bake in a greased and floured 7½ inch (19cm) round or a 2 lb loaf tin for 1 hour and 10 minutes. Leave to cool in the tin for 10 minutes. Turn out and pour the rest of the stout over the cake. Then store in tin foil for at least 2 days before serving.

Note: This cake keeps for up to one week.

Isabelle Lynch

DESSERTS

St. Multose Church

APPLE CROQUANTE
with GRANNY SMITH ICE CREAM
and SALTED BUTTER
CARAMEL SAUCE

Cristalline
1 Granny Smith apple, sliced paper thin with skin on
2 oz (55g) sugar
2 fl oz (50ml) water

Bring sugar to the boil, then cool. Coat apple slices in the cooled syrup, put on parchment paper and bake in a slow oven 110C/225F for 4 hours.

Ice Cream
4½ cups (1.25 litres) milk
3¼ Tbsp (50ml) cream
12 egg yolks
5 oz (140g) sugar
19 oz (550g) compote*

To make Compote: Peel and core 2 Granny Smith apples and place in a pan with a little water, lemon juice and a Tbsp (15ml) sugar. Cook 15 minutes and mash. Set aside. To prepare the custard, bring the milk and the cream to the boil. Beat the egg yolks together with the sugar till white. Slowly fold the egg yolk mixture into the milk and cream and cook until the candy thermometer reaches 95C. Add the apple compote. Pour into 2 bowls. Place in a pan surrounded with ice. When cool, refrigerate overnight. The next day put the mixture into an ice cream machine and follow their directions.

Caramel Sauce

2 Tbsp light brown sugar
1 Tbsp (15ml) water
1 ½ oz (40g) salted butter

Bring both to the boil, stirring until it becomes the colour of caramel (light tan). Carefully add the salted butter. Mix.

Stack the apple slices between layers of ice cream on the centre of a plate. Artistically drizzle with caramel sauce and serve.

Frederic Pastorino
Vintage Restaurant

POPPYSEED SOUFFLÉ
with a PEAR SAUCE

3¾ oz (110g) white Couverture (chocolate)
5 oz (140g) butter
8 egg yolks
6 egg whites
2 oz (55g) sugar
5 oz (140g) ground poppyseeds

1 1/3 cup (225ml) white wine
juice of ½ lemon
3 oz (85g) sugar
3 pears
4 Tbsp (60ml) Willismpear Schnapps

Preheat oven 180C/350F.

Break the Couverture into small pieces and melt slowly over a pan of hot water. Mix butter, egg yolks and half of the sugar and whisk together with the poppyseeds. Then add all the Couverture. Put the egg whites in another bowl and whisk to soft peaks. Add the sugar gradually, whisking it until the mixture is stiff. Now fold the egg whites into the Couverture mix, scooping and turning to achieve a light mass. Fill 5 buttered soufflé dishes ¾ full. Place them in a roasting tin and pour hot water into the tin to come up halfway to the side of the dishes. Bake for 20-25 minutes. Bring the sliced pears, white wine, sugar and lemon juice to the boil. Then add the Schnapps. Purée the mixture and pass it through a sieve, then chill. Serve in or out of the soufflé dish with the sauce on the side. Garnish with fresh pear.

Michael Relja
Casino House

118

BAILEY'S ICE CREAM

9 oz (250ml) cream
3 eggs
¼ cup plus 2 teas sugar
2-3 oz (50-75ml) Bailey's Irish Cream Liqueur
raspberry or strawberry coulis
Seasonal fruits to garnish

Whisk the egg whites and sugar in a large bowl until stiff. Whisk the cream in a separate bowl until firm. Mix the egg yolks and the Bailey's together. Fold this mixture into the whipped cream and then proceed to fold the egg whites into the bowl containing the egg yolk/whipped cream mixture. Freeze for 6 hours.

To Serve: Pour the strawberry or raspberry coulis over each plate. Add 2 scoops of ice cream. Garnish with fruit pieces.

Philip McEvoy
The Old Presbytery
Luxury B & B

CHOCOLATE ECLAIRS

2½ oz (70g) Oldum's cream flour
¼ pint (150ml) water
2 oz (55g) margarine
milk chocolate
pinch of salt
2 eggs, beaten
To decorate:
Whipped cream
Large bar plain chocolate

Preheat oven 220C/425F. Put the water and margarine into a saucepan over low heat until the margarine melts. Then bring to a brisk boil. Reduce heat and add sieved flour and salt. Stir briskly until it forms a soft dough and leaves the sides of the saucepan. Remove from heat and allow to cool. Add eggs and beat until the mixture is smooth and shiny. Transfer the mixture to a piping bag. Pipe 4" lengths of the mixture onto a cookie sheet 2 inches apart. Cook for about 25 minutes. Remove from oven and slit along one side. Allow to cool. Melt the chocolate in a pan over boiling water. Then spread on top of the eclairs. When the chocolate has set, fill the opening with whipped cream and refrigerate. Makes 8-10 eclairs.

Tip: When filling the mixture into the piping bag, use a 1 pint glass and set the bag into it with the top draped out over the edge of the glass. As you fill the bag, it will drop lower into the glass making it easier to fill and avoiding a mess.

Mary Collins
Impressions Hair Studio

BRIDE'S APPLE SPONGE

2 cups (450g) self-raising flour
1 cup (225g) caster (superfine) sugar
3 eggs
1 cup (250ml) vegetable oil
½ teas salt
4-5 peeled apples, chopped into large chunks

Mix all but the apples together in a bowl. Add the apples. Pour into a 9 x 12" tin. Bake for 30-40 minutes. Serve with custard, cream or ice cream.

Margot O'Leary

PARTY LUXURY APPLE PIE

Pastry to fit 9" (23cm) pie pan

Process until smooth:
8 oz (225g) marzipan
4 oz (115g) butter
2 Tbsp flour
2 eggs

Preheat oven 190C/375F.

Line the pastry with the mix. Slice 4 large apples and arrange over this mix. Sprinkle on 2 Tbsp sugar and 1 Tbsp (15ml) lemon juice. Put on the 'lid' pastry, decorate and slit. Bake between 45-50 minutes.

Croise Brogan

LEMON MOUSSE

1 brick (1 pint) vanilla ice cream
1 package lemon jelly
1 ¼ cups (300ml) boiling water
green grapes and whipped cream for garnish

Make up jelly with 1¼ cups water. Add ice cream and beat until mixed. Pour into glass flutes and chill for 6 hours. Pipe cream on each glass. Garnish with skinned and chopped green grapes.

Sheila Ryan

FAST & EASY LEMON CHEESECAKE

12 oz (350g) Philadelphia cream cheese
tin of sweet condensed milk
rind and juice of 2 lemons
9 oz (250g) digestive biscuits
4 oz (115g) butter

Put the cream cheese, milk and lemons into a bowl and "beat the bejasus out of it!!" To make the base, crush the digestive biscuits and mix with the melted butter. Press into a tin. Add the cream cheese mixture. "Voila." Refrigerate until serving.

Note: 1/3 pint of whipped cream can be added if desired.

Noel Hosford

LEMON SOUFFLÉ CUSTARD

4 eggs
2 large lemons
8 oz (225g) caster (superfine) sugar
1 oz (25g) butter
2 oz (50g) plain flour
16 fl oz (450ml) milk

Separate the eggs. Put the egg yolks, grated rind and juice of lemons, sugar, butter and flour into a food processor and blend. Add milk through funnel. Beat egg whites until stiff and fold into the liquid. Pour into a 2½ pint (140ml) greased ovenproof dish. Place the dish in a small roasting tin and pour cold water around. Cook for approximately 1 hour at 180C/350F. Serve with cream. Delicious!

Mrs. Barbara Matson

APPLE SPONGE WELCOME HOME CAKE

3 eggs
6 oz (175g) self-raising flour
6 oz (175g) caster (superfine) sugar
1 teas baking powder
6 oz (175g) soft butter or margarine
1 cooking apple
lemon curd

Preheat oven 190C/375F.

Grease a spring-form pan. Beat butter and sugar together till light. Add in eggs, then flour, sugar and baking powder. Mix just until smooth. Place in a spring-form pan. Peel apple. Slice thinly and arrange on the sponge mixture. Bake approximately ½ hour. When cool, remove from the tin. Melt 2 Tbsp (30ml) lemon curd; brush it over the cooled cake and serve.

Sheila Ryan

CHOCOLATE & RASPBERRY CHEESECAKE

8 oz (225g) chocolate
8 oz (225g) Philadelphia cream cheese
2 oz (55g) caster (superfine) sugar
10 fl oz (300ml) lightly whipped cream
1 package raspberry jelly
1 packet Jaffa cakes
½ packet digestive biscuits
4 oz (115g) butter

Crush both types of biscuits together. Melt butter and add to the biscuits. Place in the bottom of a cheesecake tin. Place in the refrigerator. Melt the jelly in microwave with ½ cup (125ml) water. Leave to cool. Melt the chocolate also. Place the cheese and the sugar in a bowl. Blend together and then add the whipped cream, blending with a spoon. Add the jelly and chocolate to the mix, then pour into the biscuit base. Leave it in the refrigerator for 1½-2 hours before serving. Add a few fresh raspberries and a sprig of fresh mint if available for decoration.

Tip: *When cutting the cheesecake, soak the knife in hot water first. This gives a nice even slice.*

Rita McKenna
An Seanachí

TIRAMISU SEMI-FREDDO

4½ oz (125 g) Jacobs Boudoir biscuits
¼ pint (150ml) strong filter coffee
8 Tbsp (120ml) Bailey's Irish Cream Liqueur,
   plus extra to serve
3 eggs, separated
2 Tbsp caster (superfine) sugar
1 lb 2 oz (500g) mascarpone cheese
5 fl oz (150ml) lightly whipped cream
cocoa powder to serve

Line a deep, freezer-proof dish with the biscuits. Mix together the coffee and 3 Tbsp (45ml) Bailey's. Pour over the biscuits and set aside. Beat the egg yolks with the sugar until pale and thick. Whisk in the mascarpone and the cream. Stir in the remaining Bailey's. Then, whisk the egg whites until soft peaks from and fold into the cream mixture. Spoon on top of the biscuits and freeze for about 2 hours. You want a just frozen, but not a hard or solid texture, pretty much like soft ice cream. Spoon into serving dishes, dust with cocoa powder and drizzle over a little extra Bailey's. Serve.

Tip: If you are not a Bailey's fan, mix together Kalhua or Tia Maria liqueur with coffee and sweeten to taste.

Anne Fitzsimons

TRADITIONAL TRIFLE

2 whole eggs plus 2 yolks or, 3 eggs
2 teas (1 desertspoon) castor sugar
1 Tbsp cornflour (cornstarch)
¾ pint milk
1 x 7" spongecake 1 inch deep, cut into squares
strawberry jam (homemade if possible)
1 tin peaches
small glass sherry or brandy
½ pint (300ml) whipped cream
chocolate flake
1-2 oz (25-55g) toasted almonds, chopped

Beat eggs, sugar and cornflour together until creamy. Heat the milk to just below boiling. Then slowly stir into the egg mixture, return to pan and cook, stirring all the time over a low heat until thick. Do not allow to boil. Cover and leave to cool but do not let it set. Meanwhile, sandwich the sponge cake together with the jam. Put the cake upside down in the bottom of a glass dish. Pour fruit juice and sherry over the sponge and leave to soak for ½ hour. When cool, pour custard over the sponge. Spread with whipped cream and top with chocolate or almonds.

Ann Marie Searls

VEGETABLES
&
MISCELLANEOUS

Maises, Pearse Street

CREAMED PARSNIPS

1½ lb (700g) parsnips
1 oz (25g) butter
4-6 oz (110-170ml) cream
nutmeg
salt and pepper

Clean and chop the parsnips. Boil in salted water until very soft. Drain and liquidize with butter and cream until you get a purée. Place in a serving dish. Grate some nutmeg on top. Put into a warm oven until ready for serving.

Ann Marie Searls

LEEK, MUSTARD & CHIVE MASH

2 lb (1kg) potatoes, peeled
8 oz (225g) baby leeks, finely chopped
3 Tbls (45ml) fromage frais
1 Tbsp coarse grain mustard
2 Tbsp chives, finely chopped
salt and freshly ground black pepper

Cook the potatoes in plenty of salted boiling water for 20-25 minutes. In a non-stick frying pan, dry-fry the leeks until soft. Drain the potatoes well and mash until smooth. Beat in the fromage frais along with the leeks, mustard and chives. Season well with salt and black pepper. Spoon into a warmed serving dish.

Anne Fitzsimons

COURGETTES with ALMOND, GINGER & CARROT STUFFING

1 large onion, peeled and chopped
2 Tbsp (30ml) olive oil
4 medium courgettes (ensure skin is free from blemishes)
1 clove garlic, minced
12 oz (350g) carrots, scraped and very finely diced
¾ teas fresh, grated ginger
4 oz (115g) flaked or nibbed almonds

Preheat oven to 190C/375F. Fry the onion in the oil in a pan for 5 minutes. Halve the courgettes lengthways, making sure that they are at room temperature. Scoop out the flesh, being careful not to break through the skin. Roughly chop the flesh and add it to the onion, garlic, carrot and ginger. Cover and sauté gently for about 10-15 minutes, or until the vegetables are cooked but not browned. Remove from the heat and add the almonds and some freshly ground pepper to taste. Arrange the courgette halves in a lightly greased casserole dish. Fill the halves with the mixture. Cover with foil and bake for about 40 minutes. Serves 4.

Note: This is a wonderful dish on its' own, as a light supper or, as a side dish to fish or chicken.

Deirdre Mullins

BRAISED RED CABBAGE

1 red cabbage, cored and shredded
1 large onion, peeled and chopped
2 Tbsp (30ml) oil
2 Tbsp (30ml) lemon juice
freshly ground black pepper to taste
pinch brown sugar

Put the cabbage in a large saucepan. Cover with water and bring to the boil. Drain thoroughly. Gently fry the onions in the oil in the same large saucepan for about 5 minutes; then add the cabbage, cover, and cook on a very low heat for 50-60 minutes, stirring every now and then to prevent catching. Just before serving, add the lemon juice and pepper to taste.

Note: If desired, a bunch of roughly chopped parsley can be added in just before serving also.

Deirdre Mullins

TOMATOES VINAIGRETTE

2 medium tomatoes, peeled and chopped
4 spring onions, chopped
1 stalk celery, chopped
1 Tbsp minced parsley
¼ cup (60ml) extra-virgin olive oil
2 Tbsp (30ml) wine vinegar
salt and pepper

Combine the tomatoes, onion, celery, parsley, oil, vinegar and seasonings. Chill for several hours before serving.
Makes about 2 cups.

Brian O'Shea

GARLIC CAULIFLOWER CHEESE

1 large cauliflower
1½ oz (40g) butter
1½ oz (40g) plain flour
1 pint (600ml) milk
2 oz (55g) Gruyére cheese, grated
3 oz (85g) mature Cheddar cheese, grated

Topping
1 oz (25g) butter, melted
2 cloves garlic, peeled and finely chopped
½ cup (100g) fresh bread crumbs

Preheat oven to 190C/375F. Remove the tough outer leaves from the cauliflower, then cut it into large florets. Bring a large pan of salted water to the boil, add the cauliflower and bring back to the boil. Reduce the heat, cover and simmer for about 10 minutes until just tender. Drain and leave to one side. Melt the butter in a saucepan, add the flour and cook for one minute, stirring constantly. Take the pan away from the heat and gradually stir in the milk. Return to the heat and cook for 3-5 minutes, stirring until thickened. Reserve 2 Tbsp of each of the cheeses and stir the remainder into the sauce. Season to taste with salt and freshly ground pepper. Place the cauliflower in a shallow ovenproof dish and pour the sauce over the top. To make the topping, mix together the melted butter, garlic, breadcrumbs and the reserved cheese; season with salt and pepper. Scatter the bread crumb mixture over the cauliflower and bake for 25-30 minutes until golden and bubbling. Serve immediately.

Jill Barry

RED ONION MARMALADE

5 Tbsp (75ml) olive oil
4 large red onions, thinly sliced
½ teas salt
2 oz (55g) demerara sugar
4 oz (115g) sultanas
½ cup (125ml) red wine
½ fl oz (12.5ml) red wine vinegar

Heat the oil in a pan over medium heat. Cook the onions.
Stir until they wilt. Lower the heat, add the salt and cook for
10 minutes. Then add the sugar and the sultanas. Season
with black pepper and cook until the sugar dissolves. Reduce
heat and simmer gently for about 1 hour until thick. Cool
slightly before pouring into clean jars.

*Note: This is excellent with spicy potato cakes, cold meat, or
salmon cakes.*

The Bulman
Summercove

RED ONION MARMALADE II

6 large red onions
3 cloves garlic
4 oz (115g) brown sugar
2½ fl oz white vinegar
2 teas freshly grated ginger
8 oz (225g) butter
1½ cups (375ml) balsamic vinegar
freshly chopped rosemary

Sweat the onions, garlic and ginger in butter. Add the sugar. Slowly caramelize very thoroughly. Add the remaining ingredients, reduce until ready to be put into clean jars.

Note: If it is too vinegary, add a little more sugar or some freshly squeezed orange juice.

Vickie McGlennon
Crackpots Ceramic Restaurant

JILL'S GRANOLA

1 cup (225g) oat bran
4½ cups (1 kg) rolled oats
1 cup (225g) coarsely chopped almonds
3 cups (675g) sunflower seeds
1 cup (225ml) canola oil
½ cup (125ml) malt syrup, or ¼ cup (60ml) honey
¾ cup (170ml) honey or ½ cup (110ml) maple syrup
1 Tbsp (15ml) vanilla
½ teas (2.5 ml) almond extract
1 ½ Tbsp cinnamon
pinch of cloves
1 ½ teas salt
1 cup (225g) each, dried apricots and dates
½ cup (115g) raisins

Preheat oven 170C/325F. Put the oats, chopped almonds and sunflower seeds in a large bowl. Combine the oil, sweeteners, vanilla, almond extract, spices and salt. Heat this mixture in a saucepan until it becomes watery. Pour the oil mixture over the dry ingredients, tossing till everything is moistened. Spread the mixture in a baking pan. Bake in the middle of the oven for 20 minutes or until the granola turns golden, stirring every 5 minutes. Transfer to a large bowl or cool in the baking pan and toss occasionally until the granola is thoroughly cool and dry. Add the dried fruit. Store in a tightly covered container.

Jill Roberts-Thompson
Tumbleweed

KITCHEN POTPOURRI

The same spices that lend so much character to cooked foods can also be kept around every day to fill the kitchen with a pleasant scent. Place the mixture in an oversized cup, a decorative bowl or a catch pot for setting out on a kitchen counter.

¼ cup (55g) whole cloves
1 cup (225g) whole allspice
10 cinnamon sticks, each 3 inches (7.5cm) long, broken into pieces
8 small bay leaves
4 whole nutmegs
3 Tbsp star anise
2 Tbsp whole cardamon pods

Combine all the ingredients in a bowl, mixing well. Store indefinitely at room temperature, stirring occasionally. **Makes about 2 cups.**

Anonymous

INDEX

To order additional copies, or to request a gift order,
please fax us at
(949) 767-5959
or to
jbergin@gillisa.com